GEORGE CATLIN
PAINTER OF THE INDIAN WEST

Portrait of George Catlin, 1848, by William Fisk. National Portrait Gallery, Smithsonian Institution. Gift of Miss May C. Kinney, Ernest C. Kinney, and Bradford Wickes, 1945.

GEORGE CATLIN
PAINTER OF THE INDIAN WEST

by
MARK SUFRIN

ATHENEUM 1991 NEW YORK
MAXWELL MACMILLAN CANADA · TORONTO
MAXWELL MACMILLAN INTERNATIONAL
NEW YORK · OXFORD · SINGAPORE · SYDNEY

Library of Congress Cataloging-in-Publication Data. Sufrin, Mark. George Catlin: Painter of the Indian West/by Mark Sufrin.—1st ed. p.   cm. Includes bibliographical references. Summary: A biography of the painter, author, and ethnographer who devoted his life to recording Indian life, not only in this country but in South America and Asia. ISBN 0-689-31608-9. 1. Catlin, George 1796–1872—Juvenile literature. 2. Painters—United States—Biography— Juvenile literature. 3. Indians of North America—Pictorial works—Juvenile literature. 4. West (U.S.) in art—Juvenile literature. 5. Catlin, George, 1796–1872. [1. Artists.] I. Title. ND237.C35S8 1991   759.13—dc20   [B]   [92] 90—19813

GEORGE CATLIN
PAINTER OF THE INDIAN WEST

Buffalo Chase in Snowdrifts, Indians Pursuing. National Museum of American Art, Smithsonian Institution. Gift of Mrs. Joseph Harrison, Jr.

ONE

IN THE BITTER WINTER OF 1852–1853, GEORGE CATLIN wandered the streets of Paris. He was fifty-six years old, alone and despairing, growing deaf, and so poor he couldn't afford firewood to warm his cheap room. Later judged a great and extraordinary American, he was now little more than a vagrant as he roamed the grand boulevards of the gray smoky city. Police eyed him with suspicion, and after one questioned him, he described Catlin as "a queer, little hollowfaced deaf fellow in a shabby greatcoat. Looks like a crank."

He had spent most of the last dozen years in Europe exhibiting his famous "Indian Gallery"—a collection of hundreds of his paintings of the untamed Plains Indians of the American West. In the early 1830s he had ventured into wild, dangerous country to paint native American nations at the height of their power and elegance. He had also displayed Indian teepees, clothes, weapons, pipes, and religious and domestic artifacts. Often he had authentic Plains Indians performing ritual dances and songs.

To record and preserve that Indian culture was a passion that haunted and obsessed him, cost him his family and health, and

1

made him a poor wanderer until he was an old man. (In 1864 he wrote to a friend: "In my whole life I was never near starving to death as now.") But he was certain his sacrifices had been made for a great purpose, for a people he admired beyond all others, a country and a people he described as:

An Indian world entirely different than anything seen or painted before——a vast country where all men are red; where meat is the staff of life; where no laws but those of honor are known; where wolves are white and bears grizzly . . . where the rivers are yellow and white men are turned savages . . . the dogs all wolves, women are slaves, men are lords uncorrupted by the vices of civilization . . . where the predominant passions of the savage breast are ferocity and honor.

I love [this] people who always made me welcome to the best they had . . . who are honest without laws, who have no jails or no poorhouse . . . a people who worship God without the Bible, for I believe that God loves them also . . . whose religion is all the same, and who are free of religious animosities . . . a people who have never raised a hand against me, or stole my property . . . who have never fought a battle with white men except on their own ground . . . a people who live and keep what is their own without lock and key . . . and oh! how I love a people who don't live for the love of money.

A brilliant success at first, a celebrity in London and Paris, the friend of nobility, artists, writers, and scientists, he had lost everything. Within a year in the mid-1840s, his wife was dead of pneumonia, his only son of typhoid. In one of his books he called their deaths "a sad twist of fate," but never once admitted that his obsession with the Indian Gallery had caused terrible hardship for his family.

In London, in the spring of 1852, Catlin's debts, wild land speculations, bad judgments, and rash ambition finally caught up with him. He had been living on credit for many years, borrowing against his collection in the hope that the U.S. government would buy it. Creditors closed in, his apartment furnishings seized, and Catlin was thrown into debtor's prison. His wife's family now thought him nothing more than eccentric and irresponsible. Gregory Dudley, Catlin's brother-in-law, came to London and took Catlin's three young daughters back to America. Catlin was released from prison at Dudley's request and fled to Paris with a few paintings, sketches, and notebooks. The Indian Gallery was to be auctioned off to pay his creditors.

However crushing his personal tragedy, his physical and financial decline, Catlin persisted. He had to save his Indian Gallery for future generations to see. He knew the Indians were doomed in the inevitable advance of the white man's civilization, "sweeping the streams and prairies all the way to the Pacific, leaving the Indians to inhabit, and at last starve upon, the dreary and solitary waste." His was the first and most complete record— some six hundred paintings of forty-eight tribes, along with his writings— of a fierce, free people. He once again petitioned the U.S. Senate to buy his collection, but was turned down by one vote, despite the support of Daniel Webster and other powerful senators.

Catlin raged when he heard that his Indian Gallery was to be broken up and sold in small lots, to be dispersed and disappear forever. Then he learned that Joseph Harrison, an American passing through London, had paid off the creditors and taken possession of the paintings and artifacts. He had the collection crated and shipped to his Philadelphia boiler works where it was stored in a basement—unseen for twenty-seven years. Catlin found some small satisfaction that his Indian Gallery was saved "for my country by an American gentleman." But he had little hope of ever recovering it unless he could repay Harrison. He wrote in his last book:

I was lost. . . . My occupation gone, and with no other means on earth than my hands and brushes, and less than half a life, at best, before me. . . . My thoughts turned to Dame Fortune, to know if there was anything yet in store for me.

To keep warm in the harsh Paris winter Catlin often went to the library called Bibliotheque Imperial. One day a seedy man sitting nearby told him of some old Spanish manuscripts he had translated. They spoke of ancient gold mines of incredible riches in the Crystal Mountains of northern Brazil. Catlin, always a dreamer and a man in pursuit of the horizon, was fascinated. *If he could find the gold mines. . . .* Denying age, illness, and deafness, he saw it as a last chance, and determined to set out on an odyssey of high adventure in the South American wilds. It was to prove an epic journey of harrowing exploration and artistic achievement.

TWO

GEORGE CATLIN WAS AMERICAN TO THE BONE. HIS AN-
cestors had lived in Litchfield, Connecticut, as early as 1664 and
became prosperous New England gentry. His grandfather and father—the latter enlisting as a drummer boy at thirteen—served
eight years in the revolutionary war against the British. In 1787
Putnam Catlin, his father, returned to Litchfield to study law. He
moved west to Wilkes Barre, Pennsylvania, to work as a lawyer,
and married Polly Sutton, the daughter of early settlers in the state
and a survivor of an Indian massacre.

George was born in Wilkes Barre on July 26, 1796, the fifth of
fourteen children. It was a rough river town, a drinking stopover
for boatmen and loggers. Brawling drunks roamed the muddy
streets. There was no church where Polly Catlin, a devout Meth-
odist, could baptize her children. A few years before, local farmers
had rebelled against a government whiskey tax, and President
George Washington had called out the militia to quell the upris-
ing. West of the Susquehanna River there was a lawless frontier
and hostile Indians, the mountains leaned to the west, wolves
howled in the moonlight, and the river was the only road.

By 1800 Putnam Catlin was in poor health and decided to abandon his legal practice. He moved his growing family forty miles across the New York border to a farm in the wilderness in Broome County. He and his older sons cleared the land and planted crops. The farm barely kept them alive, but the streams teemed with fish, and they hunted deer and small game. Despite his ignorance of farming, the father was certain his family could prosper there. He planned to provide his sons a classical education, then expected they would probably move farther west. The idea of "moving west" was already deep in the American consciousness.

Young George became fascinated by nature in that idyllic rustic life. He hunted and fished, searched for Indian relics, and explored the forest and caves. He was far more interested in becoming another Daniel Boone than in studying his schoolbooks. "The early part of my life," he later wrote, "was whiled away somewhat in vain, with books held reluctantly in one hand, and a rifle or fishing pole firmly and lovingly grasped in the other."

He heard tales from trappers and Indian fighters of the Ohio Valley and the mysterious lands of the Mississippi a long way to the west. His imagination was fired most by his mother's stories. In June 1778, during the revolutionary war, seven-year-old Polly lived with her family in Pennsylvania's Wyoming Valley. Farms were attacked by Tories (people siding with the British) and their Indian allies. The farm families took refuge in a fort near Wilkes Barre, but the Tory force broke through the colonial defenses. The Indians—Mohawk, Seneca, and Oneida—broke into the fort and massacred over three hundred men, women, and children. Polly, and her mother and father, were among the lucky few who escaped. The colonials regrouped and drove the Tories and Indians

Mrs. Putnam Catlin (Polly Sutton). National Museum Of American Art, Smithsonian Institution. Catherine Walden Myer Fund.

into central New York. Tales of the atrocities stirred George's interest in the "primitive red man." He dreamed of the day when he could follow the trails into the West.

George didn't see his first Native American until he was ten. At that time he was only allowed to use a fowling piece, a light shotgun for birds and small game. He envied his older brothers as they leveled their long smoothbore rifles and brought down deer. George was bored hunting rabbit and squirrel, and felt that hunting bigger game like deer was a passage to manhood. One day at dusk he took his brother's rifle, against his father's strict order and set out to get his deer. He hid on a ledge near the ruins of an old sawmill and watched a salt spring. A big whitetail buck suddenly appeared and headed to the spring to lick salt. Excited, George propped the rifle barrel on a rock and had his sights dead on the animal's heart. He took a deep breath, ready to squeeze off a shot. In that instant a rifle to his left cracked and the buck dropped.

Although startled, George had the sense to stay hidden. He watched as a tall Indian came out of the brush carrying a rifle. The Indian drew a knife and slit the animal's throat, then hung it by the hind legs from a tree to let it bleed. He sat down and lit a pipe, his back to the boy. Flush with fear, George kept his rifle ready. The Indian slowly turned and scanned the ledge, but gave no sign he had seen anyone. "In that momentary glance—I saw humanity," George said years later. He stayed hidden until the man had carried off the deer, then ran home, shouting that he had seen an Indian.

The local Indians had been killed or driven away years before. Nobody believed George except his mother. The next morning their farmhand said he had seen some gypsies just beyond the wheat field, and the elder Catlin thought they must be George's "Indian." But, in a far pasture they found the Indian camped with his wife and young daughter, cooking some deer meat. Putnam Catlin greeted him with a peace sign, shook his hand, and they all sat down. The Indian said his name was The Great Warrior (*On-o-gong-way*) and he was an Oneida. The pipe was passed and they smoked and talked. George told how he had the deer in his sights, and how surprised he was at The Great Warrior's shot. The Indian said he would give the boy half the meat.

When he was a boy, the Oneida said, his father had been a warrior in the Battle of Wyoming. At mention of the massacre site, George glanced at his father, but Putnam Catlin was a gen-

8

tleman and he never changed expression. The Indian said there had been many slaughters by both sides. His father's party had been driven up the Susquehanna and across the mountains to the lakes. During the retreat his father made him carry a big kettle of gold they had taken from the white people. But soldiers trapped them on the banks of the creek where the sawmill was built, and his father buried the kettle of gold before they fled. Now he had made the great journey to find it. But he recognized nothing, the fields had been plowed and many trees were gone.

When asked how big the kettle was, the Indian made a large circle. Mr. Catlin sent George back to the house for a small brass kettle turned up a few years before when a field was plowed. The Oneida examined it and said it was the same kettle—but it was not gold and seemed small now. Mr. Catlin said even a small brass kettle had its uses and the Oneida should keep it. He said they could stay and fish and hunt until he could arrange a safe route back for them. It was a long journey and an Indian family traveling alone might be in a great danger—there were white men who would murder them for sport.

George visited the camp every day. He had found a rusty iron tomahawk, and the Oneida made a new hickory handle and showed him how to throw it. He made George a hickory bow plumed with woodpecker feathers, shafted and feathered the flint arrowheads the boy had collected, and made a deerskin quiver for the arrows. But a time came when the Oneida smelled the first crisp signs of autumn. Despite the dangers of the journey home, he and his family slipped away one night. On a hook of the Catlin woodhouse he left a saddle of venison, both loins and part of the backbone. An eagle quill was set in it as a farewell.

A few days later the Oneida's body was found eight miles from the Catlin home, two rifle bullets in his head. Nothing was ever heard of the wife and daughter, and the kettle of "gold" was gone. Catlin never forgot the tragedy, the blind hate of white men toward Indians. It made him a fighter for their cause through the years even as the white man robbed them of their land and dignity and destroyed their culture. And he was to carry a reminder of the kindly Oneida to his grave.

Later George and his friends tried to master the art of throwing the tomahawk, as the Oneida had taught him. But a bad throw by one of the boys glanced off a tree and the blade cut deep into George's cheekbone, scarring the left side of his face for life. Somehow, though unable to voice it as a boy, he felt this "blooding" gave him a mysterious kinship with the Indian people, to whom he would later devote his life.

In 1808 the Catlins moved to another farm in Hop Bottom, Pennsylvania. George and two brothers were sent to an academy in Wilkes Barre for five years. They were taught classical languages, mathematics, history, logic, grammar, astronomy, rhetoric, and natural philosophy. George's knowledge of classical authors such as Homer and Virgil meant much to him when he was among the Indians of the Upper Missouri River. Many times he compared the red warriors to the ancient heroes of Greece and Rome. But what Homer and Virgil created from imagination and rich language, Catlin saw in reality.

His father decided on a law career for George despite his protests. By the time he went off to law school in Litchfield, Connecticut, in 1817, he had grown into a handsome young man, the scar adding an exotic touch to his features. At twenty-one he was five feet, eight inches tall, and weighed a wiry, athletic 140 pounds. He had a dark complexion, a shock of wavy black hair, and startling blue eyes. Later in life, when his face had weathered, he liked to think that, except for the blue eyes, he could pass for an Indian.

At that time the Litchfield school offered the best legal education in the country. Students came from every state, and from the wealthiest and most aristocratic families of the new republic. The list of prominent men who trained there—federal and state supreme court judges, senators, congressmen, lawyers, teachers, and financiers—reads like a Who's Who of early America. Catlin's brother Charles had received his law training in Wilkes Barre, but nothing was too good for George, marked for greatness by his father. He was a bright but indifferent student and remembered his time at the school as "a difficult siege with lawbooks." But he was deeply influenced by teachings of justice and equality for all men and women. He couldn't have had better inspiration for his long and lonely support of the Indian cause.

Litchfield had its compensations for a healthy young man. Many Catlin relatives still lived there and introduced him to the town's elite. There was a female academy, where "pretty, romantic young ladies receive a brushing of knowledge and the arts," said a contemporary. The students of both schools lived in the same respectable homes, and the young people mingled to flirt at meals and prayers. There were dances, church socials, and picnics. One of Catlin's cousins taught watercolor painting at the academy. When she saw George's first attempts at art she thought he had promise. She encouraged him to do a portrait of Judge Tapping Reeve, the law school's headmaster. It showed his remarkable ability to capture the character of a sitter, not just a likeness. He caught the essence of the man: the wise teacher, absent-minded eccentric, and twinkling old flirt. While in school he did his first miniature portraits, but none survived.

Catlin found time in law school to read about subjects that interested him—Indians, natural history, science, and the arts. Almost unknowingly, he seemed to be preparing himself for his destiny. Art was only a hobby at first, but he became more serious about it, developing his talent by painting and drawing for long hours. He was still torn between law and art after he completed the fourteen-month course in September 1818. He began to practice law with his brother Charles in Montrose, Pennsylvania. Business was slow and he had plenty of time to think about his future. He later recalled:

> *During the next three years another and stronger passion was getting the advantage of me—that for painting, to which all my love of the law soon gave way. And after having covered nearly every inch of the lawyer's table with penknife, pen and ink, and pencil sketches of judges, juries, culprits and spectators, I very deliberately resolved to convert my law library into paintpots and brushes, and to pursue painting as my future, and certainly more agreeable profession.*

It isn't known just when Catlin decided to switch careers and become an artist. He wanted to have his father's approval, and he knew Putnam would object. But he was determined and impetuous enough to risk the stern old man's anger. By 1821 he exhibited four miniature paintings on ivory at the Philadelphia Academy of the Fine Arts, and six more the next year. In 1823 he had a studio on Philadelphia's Market Street, the shingle reading: GEORGE CATLIN, MINIATURE PAINTER. He had no formal training

12

Self Portrait. Thomas Gilcrease Museum.

and little money, but his natural talent and vivid personality soon made him a popular artist. He became friends with noted artists—Charles Willson Peale, and his sons Rembrandt and Titian, and John Neagle—and perhaps studied with them.

13

Catlin often visited the elder Peale's Philadelphia Museum. He admired the paintings of statesmen and military commanders, the models of steam engines, looms, and sewing machines. He was interested in the lectures on science and the arts. And he was fascinated by displays of the natural world and Indian West. There were stuffed mammals, birds and fish of North America, as well as rock and mineral specimens, insect and plant life. He studied the Indian clothes, weapons, and crafts gathered by the Lewis and Clark expedition to the Pacific of 1804 through 1806. He saw his first sketches of the West, done by an artist on Major Stephen Long's journey up the Platte River to the Rockies in 1819 and 1820. They gave him the first stirrings of a great and ambitious project. But he wouldn't free himself from the demands and rewards of a commercial career for another six years.

In 1824 he became a member of the Philadelphia Academy, unusual for an artist with so little experience. His fellow artists considered him one of the better painters of miniatures. He wrote to a friend: "I have had within the last year more orders than I can handle." But his work was conventional, and he was bored and restless. He was "continually reaching for some branch or enterprise of the art on which to devote a whole lifetime of enthusiasm." He didn't want to spend his life painting fashionable people and rich merchants.

He still had no idea where his vague ambitions would carry him. But late at night he practiced a new technique, painting quickly in oils on canvas or bristol board. It would allow him to create fast life-sized portraits, large-scale landscapes, and character studies of men in groups. But he still had no notion of anything as grandiose and foolhardy as going west to record dozens of Indian tribes.

14

The vast expanse of the wilderness beyond the Mississippi intrigued him. Like many others in his time, he thought of the West, the wilderness, as a spiritual refuge, an Eden of innocence and splendid beauty. And its inhabitants, the Indians, as primitives untouched by the vices of civilization, the finest example of natural law. That was the part-myth, part-reality of the day.

THREE

CATLIN'S LATE START AS AN ARTIST MADE HIM WORK with frantic energy to catch up with his more celebrated friends. His work became more confident and polished, but he wanted to allow this imagination to run free and decided to use wilder color and a less disciplined style. He did his first painting of an Indian—the Seneca chief, Red Jacket—in 1826 at Buffalo, New York. The portrait was stunning, but too realistic for popular taste. It didn't romanticize the great warrior and orator—this was an old, bitter, defiant, whiskey-sodden man, with a torn ear and drooping eyelid, and a clenched look of hate. It was brutal, even ugly—but exact, true.

Catlin became a member of the National Academy of Design, and exhibited twelve paintings at the American Academy of Fine Arts. He traveled in New York State to do a series of landscapes of Niagara Falls, the new Erie Canal, and the West Point parade grounds. The state commissioned him to do a full-length portrait of Governor DeWitt Clinton. A critic of the day called it "the worst portrait that New York possesses," and Catlin "utterly incompetent."

The criticism stung him. He wrote to General Peter B. Porter, secretary of war, making no secret of his distaste for commercial painting. "My feelings are becoming too enthusiastic for the limited and slavish branch of the arts which I now pursue, and in which I am wasting my life for a living. . . . Life is short and I have traveled half of it without stepping off the beaten path." His great ambition, he continued, "is to become a history painter." He asked Porter for an appointment as an instructor of drawing at West Point, or if that wasn't possible, to "some little agency among the naked savages . . . the finest school for an historical painter to be found in the world . . . the finest models in Nature, unmasked and unmoving in all their grace and beauty." In two years, Catlin assured Porter:

I could return with a collection of portraits of the principal chiefs of different nations, and paintings representing all their different manners and customs, as would enable me to open such a gallery, first in this country and then in London, as would in all probability handsomely repay me for my labors and afford me the advantage of such a successful introduction beyond the Atlantic.

Catlin's desire to paint the Indians was noble and sincere, but there might have been other motives. He was always an ambitious man and was desperate for success. If he felt no challenge in his work, he also had some doubts about his ability to compete with better-known, better-trained artists. Between 1820 and 1830 there were, perhaps, more good portrait painters in the country than any time before or after. But if Catlin feared the competition of other artists, it didn't make his later accomplishments any less heroic. He wanted to try his hand at fresh work and escape the

17

restrictions of an ordinary career. In his writings he insisted that his work not be judged on artistic merit, but as a record of a vanishing race.

A few years earlier he had seen a delegation of Plains Indians passing through Philadelphia en route to Washington, D.C., "arrayed and equipped in all their classical beauty, with shield and helmet, with tunic and cloak, tinted and tassled, exactly for a painter's palette! In silent and stoic dignity, these lords strutted about the city, wrapped in their pictorial robes, with their brows plumed with the quills of war eagles. . . ."

Catlin's romantic memory was such that on the spot his imagination was flamed, and he came to an instant decision:

Man, in the simplicity and loftiness of his nature, unrestrained and unfettered by the disguises of art, is surely the most beautiful model for the painter—and the country from which he hails is unquestionably the best study or school of arts in the world . . . and the history and customs of such a people, preserved by pictorial illustrations, are themes worthy the lifetime of one man—and nothing short of the loss of my life shall prevent me from visiting their country, and of becoming their historian.

He was determined, he said, to reach and record every Indian tribe on the North American continent. He would bring home portraits of their "principal personages . . . views of their villages and games, and full notes on their character and history." He also planned to "secure their costumes, and a complete collection of their manufactures and weapons, and to perpetuate them in a *Gallery Unique* for the use and instruction of future ages."

Catlin's plan to go west included his brother Julius, eight years younger and very close to him. Julius, a skilled amateur artist, shared his brother's dream. He already had experience among the Plains Indians. A graduate of West Point, he was serving as a second lieutenant at Fort Gibson in the Southwest—the domain of the Comanche, Kiowa, Apache, and Pawnee. Julius resigned from the army to accompany his brother, but their dream was delayed. When Julius arrived back east he found George too busy with portrait commissions to get away.

Catlin traveled to many cities to paint his subjects. He spent much time in Albany, New York's capital, and was often a guest at the Governor's mansion. At one reception, he met Clara Gregory, the daughter of a wealthy Albany family. A sweet-natured, pretty girl of twenty-one, she was captivated by the dashing, handsome Catlin. She loved sharing his quick enthusiasms, and his talk of plans and projects. He courted her with passion, and they were married in June 1828.

That summer was one of Catlin's happiest. Julius came to Albany and brought Indian curios he'd collected. Catlin was fascinated—it was the first time he could touch and examine objects of a people he'd already claimed for his own. The brothers and the bride went on steamboat river parties and rattled through the countryside in "splendid red and yellow stagecoaches" to visit nearby Indian reservations.

Catlin finished a copy of his Clinton portrait for the Franklin Institute of Rochester, New York. Julius delivered it, then went north of the city to sketch the falls of the Genesee River. To get a better view of the falls from below, he swam out into the tail of the whirlpool. A lone bystander said he heard a sudden yell for help, then saw a struggling man go under. The coroner called it an accidental drowning.

It was the first of many bitter tragedies that George Catlin would endure. He loved Julius above all his brothers and sisters, and suffered terrible guilt because he had sent him to Rochester. The loss cut like a wound, but it strengthened his resolve to journey west. It would be a tribute to his dead brother.

He painted reservation Seneca, Oneida, Mohegan, and Tuscarora. But he was depressed by the poor, miserable Indians contaminated by contact with white society. Wild, free Indians lay beyond the Mississippi. He was growing anxious—the frontier was rapidly moving westward. Congress was about to pass an Indian Removal Act that would force woodland tribes across the Mississippi. Steamboat travel was increasing. A national road was being built out across Ohio and Indiana to Vandalia, Illinois. New states were being carved out of the territories. Construction was beginning on the Baltimore & Ohio Railroad tracking west. The first explorers of the west had called it "a Great American Desert . . . unfit for white people . . . unfit for cultivation." But now there was a more optimistic feeling in the surge west: "A virgin continent awaits the plow."

If he was to realize his dream—if he would preserve for future generations the character of "free" Indian nations, catch them in the bloom of their primitive elegance—he would have to hurry before they, too, were corrupted by civilization.

Before he could start west in the fall of 1829, Catlin fell sick with a bad cough and "weak chest." He suffered all his life from weak lungs. His long, exhausting trips in wild lands, well into middle age, were to be a triumph of spirit and obsession over body.

Then Clara caught the "ague," a fever that brought chills and fits of shivering. They went south to escape the harsh upstate New York winter.

In Richmond, Virginia, he painted a miniature of Dolly Madison, wife of former president James Madison. She nursed Clara while Catlin did a painting of all 101 delegates to the Virginia Constitutional Convention. The painting was evidence of Catlin's frustration—outsized heads on small, scrawny bodies, like so many black-feathered, white-throated birds. It was the last straw for Catlin. He dared not delay another year. He began to make plans, said he had to go "before the West is gone."

Clara needed a long rest and he took her to her father's house in Albany. He would rejoin her when ice closed the western rivers. In the spring of 1830 he went to Washington to get the letters of introduction he needed in the West. General Porter's letter to General William Clark was the most important. Clark was Governor of the Missouri Territory and Superintendent of Indian Affairs, the man most experienced in western travel and most knowledgeable about the Plains Indians. Catlin also had letters to "the commander of every military post and every Indian agent on the western frontier."

Clara was the perfect mate for Catlin. She encouraged him, and as long as she lived she faithfully supported him in the great purpose of his life. But her family and his objected that he was deserting his wife and responsibilities, giving up a respectable career for a crazy adventure. Catlin was a stubborn man and nothing would change his plans. He had many virtues—integrity, courage, perseverance, innocence, affection for family, a striking personality. But he came first; his greatest fault was his egotism. Despite his love for Clara, he always acted in his own interest. He also made rash decisions and reasoned later—often to his sorrow.

21

Clara Bartlett Gregory Catlin (Mrs. George). National Museum of American Art, Smithsonian Institution. Catherine Walden Myer Fund.

I opened my views to my relatives and friends, but got no word of encouragement or help. I tried fairly and faithfully, but it was in vain to reason with those whose anxieties were ready to fabricate every difficulty and danger that could be imagined, without being able to understand the extent of importance of my designs—and I broke with them all—from my wife and aged parents—myself my only adviser and protector.

In the early summer of 1830 Catlin boarded an Ohio River steamboat in Cincinnati. The passage took him southwest to Cairo, Illinois, where the Ohio flowed into the Mississippi, then up the great river to St. Louis. The last night before reaching that frontier town, Catlin was too excited to sleep and paced the deck. At dawn, as the steamboat swung toward shore, his heart pounded. St. Louis was the gateway to the West—the boundary between civilized history and the primitive peoples of the Great Plains.

F O U R

ST. LOUIS WAS A BOOMING, BUSTLING RIVER TOWN OF almost eight thousand people. It was headquarters for the fur companies, traders, trappers, hunters, and adventurers pushing the frontier trade and conquest of the West. The first settlers would not start their wagons along the Oregon Trail until 1842. St. Louis was also headquarters for the Army of the West and Northwest.

Catlin was fascinated as he walked through the narrow, cobbled streets. Before reaching his hotel he heard Spanish and French, cadences of Virginia gentlemen, Ohio farmboys turned soldiers, Scotch Highlander and Irish, several Sioux dialects, Cheyenne, Crow, and Pawnee. He never imagined such a motley collection of people—grizzled trappers in dirty leather shirts and leggings, whiskered men in tall beaver hats and frockcoats, rakish river men who looked like pirates, spare-looking Yankees, merchants, and sharp-faced loungers. He seemed unaware that the crowd also included a cast of players found in any frontier boomtown—confidence men, sneak thieves, shysters, prostitutes, violent toughs, embezzlers, and murderers fleeing the law.

Seeing all these characters in St. Louis, he realized how naive he had been. Many of these hardy people had already traveled in Indian country. He had known of the fur trade and trappers working throughout the West, but had preferred to maintain the illusion of the plains as a primeval region. The land still was, perhaps, untouched by plow and unfenced. The wind still blew across endless miles of grass, and buffalo grazed by the millions. But he wondered how "his" Indians had been affected. Were they still fierce and free? Had he waited too long?

Freight wagons rolled down to warehouses on the wharves. The waterfront teemed with sternwheelers, sidewheelers, flush-deckers, old keelboat freighters, and two-story New Orleans packets. Wood smoke from the stacks floated across the low, drab buildings. Slaves carried bales of stinking, greasy beaver skins aboard the boats. The precious cargo eventually ended up in New York, Paris, London, Berlin, and St. Petersburg, Russia. Beaver trapped in icy streams were a source of wealth for St. Louis. Men everywhere wore high hats made of beaver; and the skin was also used for coats, muffs, and other accessories. But in ten years the beaver-skin hat would be replaced by hats of silk from another continent.

Heading upriver for trade with the Indians who ruled beaver and buffalo country were other goods:

Blankets in blue, green, scarlet, and white; colored glass beads, axeheads, iron pots, scalping knives, scarlet "chief's coats" (a copy of a Lieutenant General's uniform), tobacco, sugar, clay pipes, rifle balls, musket and rifle flints, short smoothbore muskets, calico shirts, white cotton stockings, steel animal traps, garters, children's bootees, bells and mirrors, and steel needles. ("Once a squaw used a steel needle," said a trapper, "she'd never go back to the bone awl.")

But the most important item of trade was whiskey. The fur companies wanted to get the Indians addicted. Indians seemed to have little tolerance for alcohol as they had never brewed their own. But once they had a taste, many would give or do anything for it. The feeling was like the religious ecstacy produced by their fasting and ritual dances. Traders made "Indian whiskey" from alcohol boiled with river water. It became a violent mixture with added substances like ginger, gunpowder, chewing tobacco, molasses, red peppers, and, occasionally, strychnine. Profits were enormous. The going rate for a stack of beaver pelts or a buffalo robe was about a half-pint of whiskey. There were drunken fights, stabbings, clubbings, and adulteries. Some Indians, sick and staggering, were still so desperate for more drink that they offered to trade their women and horses.

Catlin was perhaps the first prophet of the effect of whiskey and trinkets on the Indians. He wrote of "voracious white men debauching and robbing the primitives, sweeping the prairies all the way to the Pacific, leaving the Indians to inhabit, and at last starve upon, the dreary and solitary waste."

In St. Louis, however, Catlin was about to start on an adventure. He presented his letter of introduction to General William Clark. He also brought portraits and sketches done on the New York reservations. Clark, then sixty, was an American hero. Almost thirty years before he had explored, with Meriwether Lewis, the vast expanse of land gained from the French in the Louisiana Purchase. They followed the Missouri River to its source, then continued on to the shores of the Pacific. Now Clark was the ruler of the West. No white man could travel, trade, or trap there without his permission. No expedition could be mounted, no company formed, no treaty made with a tribe unless he approved.

He liked Catlin's Indian paintings better than any he had seen. He was also impressed that Catlin didn't ask for financial help from the government. Clark was certain the determined artist would go into Indian country even if he didn't get official approval. He admired Catlin, sat for a portrait, and became his friend and patron. Clark slyly suggested to the rich of St. Louis that Catlin paint them, and the money kept Catlin going. When tribal chiefs visited, Clark made sure Catlin was present. He was pleased to notice that the chiefs instinctively liked and trusted him. Catlin would work fast on rough portraits of the chiefs, and his sharp memory for details allowed him to finish them later.

Clark taught him the lore of the Plains Indians, their warring nature, the importance and power of chiefs and "medicine" men in tribal society. On a large map he pointed out the locations of the tribes. He said there were many different nations, composed of "clans" or "bands," following different ways of life. Along the fertile eastern edge of the plains were the farmer-hunters— Caddo, Omaha, Osage, Oto, Ponca, Wichita, Iowa, Missouri, and Kansas. Farther west were the nomad warriors who lived by hunting—Sioux, Cheyenne, Crow, Blackfeet, Arapaho, Pawnee, Assiniboin, Arikara, Comanche, and Kiowa. They were a vigorous people who had learned to come to terms with the harsh land and build an existence based on the horse and buffalo. The hard life of the plains had eliminated the weak and the misfits. These were the tribes Catlin hungered to paint.

Before 1840 Indians were the rulers of the Great Plains. A few army posts were stretched thinly along the eastern edge, and a

27

Old Bear, a Medicine Man. National Museum of American Art, Smithsonian Institution. Gift of Mrs. Joseph Harrison, Jr.

scattering of trading posts were lost in the boundless expanse of prairie. No plow had yet cut a furrow in its millions of acres of sod. It was still a land of the Indian and buffalo, and for many years remained a lonely and forbidding place for explorers and settlers moving west.

The Great Plains were fifteen hundred miles long and six hundred miles wide. They roughly covered an area including parts or all of these present states: Montana, North and South Dakota, Wyoming, Nebraska, Kansas, Colorado, New Mexico, Oklahoma, and Texas. The eastern edge had plentiful rain and the grass grew taller than a man's head. Catlin said that once on horseback he had to stand in the stirrups to see above it. The western part had a drier climate and the grass was only a few inches high, but thick.

It was a region of many rivers and little woodland. In places the plains were flat, in others, gently rolling, broken occasionally by bluffs, canyons, and nightmare badlands. It was a land of violent extremes of climate—burning summer heat and bitter winter cold. It had long droughts and savage thunderstorms, killing blizzards and explosive tornadoes. Space there seemed infinite: sweeping vistas and a sky with smoky, multicolored puffs of clouds.

It abounded in wild life—antelope, elk, badger, deer, wolverine, coyote, cougar, sage grouse, turkey, muskrat, birds and prairie dogs in the millions, grizzly bears on the high western plains, and herds of wild horses roamed the short grass. But to the Indian hunter, the buffalo was the supreme game. Gigantic herds moved like darkening seas across the plains, an estimated 15 million animals. The buffalo meant food, clothing, and shelter, and dozens of other things. It was a gift from the Creator, the Indians thought, an animal endowed with supernatural powers.

Wounded Buffalo, Strewing His Blood over the Prairie. National Museum of American Art, Smithsonian Institution, Gift of Mrs. Joseph Harrison, Jr.

In July 1830 Catlin accompanied Clark to Fort Crawford on the Upper Mississippi River. Clark supervised a treaty council with Missouri, Iowa, eastern Yankton Sioux, Omaha, and the Sauk and Fox. The latter had only recently combined into one powerful tribe. The Indians were to decide on the sale of their lands to the United States government. Black Hawk and Running Fox (*Kee-o-kuk*) were chiefs of the Sauk and Fox. Running Fox signed the treaty, but Black Hawk refused. His resistance led to the Black Hawk War—actually the forced removal of the Sauk and Fox west of the Mississippi.

For Catlin it was the beginning of his pictorial record of western Indians in their native element. In the fall he went up the Missouri to Fort Leavenworth, then the most remote army post on the river. Catlin painted No Heart (*Notch-ee-ming-a*), an Iowa chief, and the Open Door (*Ten-squat-a-way*), a Shawnee prophet and brother of the famous Tecumseh. He also painted Potawatomie and Kickapoo. In the country of the Kansas tribe he made one of his most charming paintings: a group of four warriors in elaborate dress, with a woman and child.

In the field, Catlin painted quickly and wasted no time on preliminary sketches. The outlines of the face and figure were done in broad strokes. If he had time he began to fill in costume details. Paint was applied in a thin coat, so the canvas would dry quickly and not crack when rolled into a metal cylinder.

He had faults as an artist: bad perspective and proportions, crude technique, and no training in anatomy. Catlin could define the character of an Indian's face with the greatest truth, but didn't do figures well. To save time he often ignored hands, and the scale of arms and legs was sometimes wrong. But his seated subjects often have grace, dignity, and authority. And his standing figures seem ready to spring into action.

He used only about twelve colors, but mixed his palette with dash and drama. As he traveled among the Indians, his talent and confidence grew. He seemed inspired by them and their exotic costumes. On the Upper Missouri he used much bolder color to record the varieties and excitements of savage life.

Other artists—better trained and superb technicians—followed Catlin into the West. Their work was sophisticated, often breathtaking. But none had Catlin's mission to paint a documentary record of Indian life. He painted what he saw before him, with no sweetening. His paintings have a sense of urgency, sympathy, and melancholy that the others missed.

He returned east in the late fall of 1830, but by January 1831 he was back in St. Louis. In the early spring he was off on another journey. Catlin and Major John Dougherty, an Indian agent, went up the Platte River and on through the Rocky Mountain passes to the Great Salt Lake (present Utah). According to his journals, he painted tribesmen of the Platte region. Three of his most striking portraits were of The Buffalo Bull (*La-doo-ke-a*), a Grand Pawnee warrior, He Who Strikes Two At Once (*No-way-sug-gah*), an Oto warrior, and the Big Elk (*Om-pah-ton-ga*), a chief of the Omahas. But scholars of his work think the paintings may actually have been done later, possibly 1833, when his work had greatly improved. Catlin covered an astonishing amount of territory in his years in the West. But in his writings he was careless and scrambled the sequence of his travels.

Catlin went east again. He returned to St. Louis in December 1831. A pattern seemed to be emerging in his life. After a season of intense fieldwork painting dozens of portraits, he went home to finish them with the aid of his memory and notes. He went on short trips to paint Indians in the region, and those passing through on their way to Washington, D.C. But now he was ready to paint the Indians he admired most in their own kingdom and make a written record of their lives. The great accomplishments and the great adventure were still to come.

Catlin had met Pierre Chouteau on his first trip to St. Louis. Chouteau was the western manager of John Jacob Astor's powerful American Fur Company, and ruled all the company's trading posts along the Missouri and Platte rivers. The company wanted to spread its domination northwest to the Upper Missouri. A 130-

Buffalo Bill, a Pawnee Warrior. National Museum of American Art, Smithsonian Institution. Gift of Mrs. Joseph Harrison, Jr.

foot steamboat was being prepared for a pioneering voyage. Called the *Yellowstone,* she was a wide double-deck two-stacker. She was to carry a great load of supplies and trade goods two thousand miles up the Missouri to the mouth of the Yellowstone River. Fort Union, the company's most remote trading post, had been built there. From Fort Union, trappers and traders fanned out into the still little-known territories of the Blackfeet, Crow, Sioux, Arikara, and Assiniboin. As early as 1819 a steamboat had reached Council Bluffs (present Iowa). From there the cargo had to be carried overland by packhorse or dragged upriver in keelboats, because of the Yellowstone's swift current. It was slow and expensive.

Chouteau promised Catlin a place on the *Yellowstone.* The steamboat wasn't scheduled to leave for some time, so Catlin once more went east to spend time with Clara and work on his paintings. He returned to St. Louis in March 1832. The boat would leave as soon as the ice broke up in order to take advantage of the high water. Catlin developed an exciting plan:

He would stay on the steamboat to her final stop upriver. Then his travels were to be by foot, horse, and canoe. He would explore deep into the unmapped wilderness, paint every Indian he could reach. On the voyage home, he planned a leisurely trip downriver by canoe to St. Louis, painting forts, Indian villages, and landscapes along the way.

It was to prove the most fascinating summer of his career—a four-thousand-mile odyssey among the primitive tribes of the Upper Missouri.

FIVE

THE *YELLOWSTONE* DEPARTED ST. LOUIS ON MARCH 26, 1832. Sailing with Catlin were Pierre Chouteau and Major John Sanford, an Indian agent. Sanford was escort for Pigeon's Egg Head (*Wi-jun-jon*), son of an Assiniboin chief. He was returning from Washington, D.C., where he met President Andrew Jackson. When he left his village, the Assiniboin was dressed in fine buckskin clothes adorned with scalps of his enemies. On his return he was a far different-looking man. "In Washington," said Catlin,

> he had exchanged his beautifully decorated costume for full military dress trimmed with gold lace and epauletes. On his head was a high-crowned beaver hat with a huge red feather. . . . His feet were pinched into high-heeled boots, which made him walk like a yoked hog. A large silver medal on a blue ribbon hung from his neck, and he wore a sword. On his hands he wore kid gloves, and in them held a blue umbrella in one and a large fan in the other. . . .

Catlin did a witty "before and after" painting of Pigeon's Egg Head, showing the change. "In this fashion," he said, "was the

35

Pigeon's Egg Head, Going to and Returning from Washington. National Museum of American Art, Smithsonian Institution. Gift of Mrs. Joseph Harrison, Jr.

poor Indian transformed, whistling 'Yankee Doodle' as he stood upon the deck of the steamer taking him home. There he was soon to light his pipe, and cheer the teepee fireside with tales of novelty and wonder." Catlin later told of the Assiniboin's humiliating return to his home village.

A colorful group of adventurers crowded the two decks of the ship. Most were employees of the American Fur Company— rough, picturesque French-Canadian river men, Yankee trappers of English and Scottish stock, and half-breeds who did much of the manual labor. Besides the usual cargo of trade goods, the *Yellowstone* carried two hundred fifty gallons of alcohol by special permit of General Clark. Congress had put severe restrictions on the shipment of whiskey to the Indians. Clark, superintendent of Indian affairs in the West, was expected to enforce the ban. But he was financially involved in the Indian trade and pretended he had received no official notice. He gave permission for the last two hundred fifty gallons of legal alcohol to be shipped aboard the steamboat.

For Catlin, the voyage was a dream realized. The wooded banks were greening, lit with redbud and dogwood. Cranes and geese flew across the fiery dawns, and curious birds circled the boat. He and other passengers often explored the countryside on foot, perhaps crossing some green peninsula almost encircled by the winding river. Sometimes they debarked to man the ropes that hauled the boat off sandbars. On the way upriver Catlin painted landscapes, Indian villages, scenes of Indian life, and portraits.

The *Yellowstone* put in at a Ponca village near the mouth of the Niobrara River (present Nebraska). This was a transition area for the western Indians' culture. Beyond that point, the tribes had been little affected by advancing white civilization. The Ponca

37

were near enough to the frontier to be threatened by whiskey and smallpox. They were preparing to move their village farther west, where game was plentiful. Said Catlin:

> *I saw a very aged and emaciated man of the tribe who was being left behind. Once a distinguished chief, he was now too old and feeble to travel. He was being left to starve, or meet such death as was his fate, possibly wolves. Almost naked, he sat by a small fire, with a few sticks of firewood and a buffalo skin stretched over his head—with only a few half-picked bones and a dish of water within reach, but no weapons. I could only shake his hand, and he smiled, aware that I was a white man and that I sympathized with his misfortune.*

Before he left, Catlin painted their chief, the Smoke. Using a reference to a classic Roman, he described him as a "Caius Marius weeping over the poverty of his ill-fated community." But his sadness over the Ponca soon left him as the *Yellowstone* forged northwest.

The trip up the muddy, swirling Missouri was an adventure in itself. Erosion constantly undermined the river banks. Trees, large bushes, and rocks became dangerous obstacles, hard to spot in the dark water. The boat stopped many times so the crew could cut away some of the debris below the surface. Each night the boat was moored at an inlet or island. Daylight was needed to steer through ever-changing channels and past sandbars and obstacles.

During stops, woodcutters searched for fuel, and hunters brought in waterfowl, deer, antelope, and eventually, buffalo. Trade goods were unloaded at various fur company posts along the way. The stops were short—the shallows ahead could only be navigated if they caught floodwaters from melting snow. All the while, Catlin sketched local tribesmen as they gaped at "The Great Medicine Canoe with Eyes."

As the boat steamed upriver, fruit trees, wildflowers, and tall grass were left behind. Catlin wrote his vivid impressions of the great river in spring flood:

> *It is different in appearance and character from all other rivers in the world. We felt a terror the moment we entered its waters from the Mississippi. The boiling waters of the Missouri sweep off in one unceasing current. In all of the 2,000 miles there is scarcely an eddy or resting place for a canoe. The rich soil of its banks continually falls away, and the water is always filled with sediment and always opaque. At all seasons it is the color of coffee or chocolate with some cream stirred in . . . a silver coin cannot be seen through an eighth of an inch of Missouri water.*

After the first one thousand miles, the journey became an expedition into untamed land. The heavily loaded steamboat struggled against the swollen current. Herds of buffalo, elk, and other game fled in confusion at the sound and smell of the *Yellowstone*'s puffing. Cannons being taken to Fort Union were fired at the approach to every large Indian village. Some Indians pressed their faces to the ground and cried out to the Great Spirit. Some hurried to kill their favorite horse as a sacrifice to appease their angry God. Many fled in fear to the distant hills. When they realized the boat was no threat, they returned to the shore, smiling and waving.

While Catlin sketched on deck, he heard talk that disturbed him. He learned just how greedy and cynical the fur traders were. They discussed how many beaver skins to demand for a bottle of cheap whiskey, and how much they could dilute it and still get

*Big Bend on the Upper Missouri,
1900 Miles above St. Louis.*
National Museum of American
Art, Smithsonian Institution.
Gift of Mrs. Joseph Harrison, Jr.

Indians drunk. He heard them argue the best way to get Indians to kill many buffalos, and how few trade goods they would give in return. If Catlin ever had any doubts about the Indians' fate, he was certain now. Their way of life was doomed, making him more determined to be their pictorial historian and to fight for their cause. And he was drawing closer to the realization of his dream. The *Yellowstone* was steaming into the heart of Sioux country.

At one point the river ran so low, the boat's shallow keel was grounded in midchannel. There was no chance of going on until the river rose. Catlin joined Pierre Chouteau and seventeen men in a long march. They were bound for Fort Pierre, named for Chouteau, at the joining of the Missouri and Teton rivers. Catlin heard there was a large party of Sioux camped there: "I packed on the backs of several men such articles for painting as I might want . . . with my sketchbook slung on my own back, and my rifle in hand."

The exhausting march gave Catlin a chance to test himself against traders and trappers who had lived rough in the wilds for years. He wanted to get accustomed to mocassins, but at the end of the first day he "felt like giving up the journey and throwing myself on the ground in hopeless despair." A half-breed taught him to toe-in as he walked and it quickly made him more comfortable. They reached Fort Pierre on May 23 and saw hundreds of Sioux teepees outside the stockade. But just as they arrived, Catlin saw something that "disgusted" him.

The Sioux had spotted an immense buffalo herd on the west bank of the Missouri. They forded the river at noon, returning to the fort at sundown with fourteen hundred buffalo tongues, which were exchanged for a few gallons of whiskey. "Not a skin or pound of meat, except the tongues, was brought in . . . an exhibition of the rash character of the Indians, and his recklessness in catering to his appetite, as long as inducements are held out for its gratification." Catlin would learn that Indians were as wasteful as whites—unwary accomplices in their own destruction.

Indians often killed buffalo just to get at the cut of meat they liked most. "Each man selects the part of the animal that best suits his own taste, and leaves the rest to decay or be eaten by wolves and coyotes." Often they killed just for sport. The plains were littered with half-butchered buffalos. Catlin's vision of the "noble savage" weakened when he saw how they could waste and destroy. He had thought they treated the land and animal life with great respect. The truth, however, destroyed his illusions.

Many tribes were born wasters. They killed all the game in a region and had to move on to fresh hunting grounds. They destroyed great numbers of cottonwood trees, cutting off the bark to feed their horses in winter. In autumn they set fire to prairie grass to insure an early growth of new grass in the spring. The fires swept across the country for one hundred miles, burning belts of precious timber and doing other damage.

It was a valuable lesson for Catlin. He would not romanticize the Indians. And he wouldn't flinch from recording—in paint and words—Indian cruelty, waste, and sadistic religious rites. Above all, he had to be honest. Now he was entranced by the notorious Sioux:

I am in the heart of the country of the Sioux or Dakota, a word meaning 'allies.' This tribe is one of the most numerous in North America and one of the most warlike, numbering some 40- or 50,000. . . . Their personal appearance is fine and fascinating, tall and straight and graceful. . . . The Sioux are a migrating tribe divided into forty-two bands or clans, each with its own chief. Among the most powerful bands are the Oglala, Brulé, Hunkpapa, Minneconju and San Arc. . . .

SIX

BECAUSE THE STEAMBOAT HAD SUCH DIFFICULTY NAVI-
gating the Missouri, Catlin's stay at Fort Pierre was longer than
expected. Next to Fort Union, it was the most important trading
post on the river. It lay midway between St. Louis and the mouth
of the Yellowstone River.

Newly built, the fort was 325 feet by 340 feet, surrounded by
an 18-foot long stockade. Inside were storage buildings, stables,
and living quarters. There were two blockhouses on the wall from
which a man could scan the prairie for miles. From that high
perch, Catlin saw the lack of landmarks—not a tree, shrub, or
elevation on the endless grass. He understood why the early Span-
iards traveled as they did. To keep from marching in circles, they
shot an arrow directly ahead and marched to it, then another, and
another.

The captain of the fort was a fiery-tempered Scotsman named
William Laidlaw. He ranked only second to Kenneth McKenzie,
captain of Fort Union, who was called "King of the Upper Missouri." Laidlaw, Catlin noted, occupied spacious and comfortable
quarters, which were "well-supplied with the comforts and lux-

uries of life. It is neatly and respectably conducted by a fine-looking, modest and dignified Sioux woman, the kind and affectionate mother of his flock of pretty and interesting children."

Catlin quickly discovered that most of the men who had forged beyond the frontier lived with Indian women. A woman who got a white husband or lover was considered lucky. A white man most often treated her with a consideration unknown to Indian custom. She bore his children and worked for him, and in return she gained respect and wealth beyond her reach. She had raised her status and was the envy of other Indian women.

McKenzie had come down from Fort Union. For the Indians, the arrival of the steamboat, and the presence of one of the most important fur company officials, prompted a great celebration. Catlin watched the Sioux in a festival of competitive games, horse races, dances, and religious ceremonies. It seemed to him like "a wild and primitive country fair." From daylight to dark and long into the night, he heard the pounding of drums and the wild chants and yells and songs of the dancers.

Catlin painted the Indian hunting buffalo. The big, humpbacked animals roamed in herds of up to hundreds of thousands that could cover the plains from horizon to horizon. A man could ride through a herd from sunup to sundown and still be in its midst. One man said he rode one hundred miles through a herd.

The Indian stripped himself of anything that might hinder him on the hunt. He held his bow and five or six arrows in his left hand ready for instant use. His horse was trained to approach the animal from the right side so he could shoot to his left. The hunter aimed at the heart, the arrow piercing deep—"to the feather." Buffalos were exceptionally placid animals. But once they caught the scent of man, or saw any unusual or rapid movement, they stampeded. To keep a herd from panicking, Indians often approached upwind on foot to within certain bowshot—fifty to one hundred yards. They sometimes wore wolfskins as disguise, as Catlin once painted himself and Indians on the hunt. On horse the Indians cut animals out of the herd so they could approach without being trampled to death. A good horse could usually outrun a buffalo, but it had to go at full gallop, and there was the chance it might break down before the buffalo did.

Catlin once wounded a large bull. The dying animal staggered away and he followed until it suddenly turned. At that point he drew his notebook and began sketching the wounded bull, which "stood stiffened up . . . swelling with awful vengeance." Catlin circled the animal to observe its "numerous attitudes." When it finally collapsed, Catlin threw his hat at it, "rousing him on his legs, rallying a new expression, and I sketched him again." He had to harass the dying beast, he said, so he could make the first authentic paintings of buffalo.

Buffalo hunts were a means of displaying the power and endurance of the animal and the courage of his Indian pursuer. They were high drama on the plains, a raw test in primitive survival. The buffalo was pitted against the hunter in a race to the death. Usually the Indian was victorious, but when he suffered defeat it was usually bloody and painful.

Catlin's main purpose, though, was to record the faces and costumes of the Sioux and he set up a painting studio in a tent. His first subject was Chief One Horn (*Ha-won-je-tah*). He was the greatest hunter of the Hunnecoyi band, and had taken many scalps in battle. His white elkskin shirt, Catlin noted, "is fringed with a profusion of porcupine quills and scalplocks. His hair is very long and divided into two parts, and lifted up and crossed over the

Catlin and His Guide Approaching Buffalo under White Wolf Skins. National Museum of American Art, Smithsonian Institution. Gift of Mrs. Joseph Harrison, Jr.

One Horn, Head Chief of the Miniconjou Tribe. National Museum of American Art, Smithsonian Institution. Gift of Mrs. Joseph Harrison, Jr.

head with a simple tie, giving it somewhat the appearance of a Turkish turban."

Catlin invited other chiefs to look at the painting of One Horn. They had never seen a lifelike portrait before. They clasped their hands over their mouths in fright and amazement. They were so astonished at Catlin's magic, they gave him the name the Medicine Painter. Sioux medicine men denounced the portrait. They said it would bring bad luck and early death to anyone permitting their face and body to be put in such a form. "He can't even sleep at night," they said, because the "eyes were always open." If Catlin merely glanced at a warrior, he quickly slipped away. But One Horn was finally convinced by Catlin that no harm would come to him, that it was really a great honor. He told his people that Catlin had come a great distance just to paint the great men of the Sioux and was going to take them home for the white chiefs to see.

His next subjects were the Black Rock (*Ee-ah-sa-pa*), and the Tobacco (*Tchan-dee*), a powerful Oglala chief. When he casually asked to paint a woman, the chiefs were first amused, then angry. Paint a woman? What had she done? She had never taken a scalp or hunted the buffalo. She only built fires and dressed animal skins and gossiped with other women. Later, a party of Cheyenne, friendly with the Sioux, rode in. Among them was a handsome woman, She Who Bathes Her Knees (*Tis-se-woo-na-tis*). The Cheyenne, less rigid, puritanical, and haughty than the Sioux, were quick to grant permission to paint her.

The Sioux braves were eager to have their portraits painted once they were assured it was safe. Catlin was amused by their conceit, but aware they still had some superstitious doubt:

The vanity of these men is beyond description. An Indian often lays down from morning to night in front of his portrait, admiring the beautiful face, and faithfully guarding it from accident or harm . . . owing to their belief that there may be life to a certain extent in the picture, and that if harm or violence be done to it, it may in some mysterious way affect their health or do them other injury.

When not painting, Catlin talked with fur company officials, traders, and trappers to learn all he could of Indian life. Far into the night he made notes for his book, and wrote letters to be published in the *New York Commercial Advertiser*.

Catlin, McKenzie, Laidlaw, Chouteau, and Major Sanford were guests at a Sioux feast featuring dog meat held in a large semicircular tent formed by combining two teepees. One Horn rose and spoke to Sanford, the government agent:

My father, we offer you today not the best we have—for we have plenty of good buffalo hump and marrow. But we give you our hearts in this feast. We have killed our faithful dogs to feed you—and the Great Spirit will seal our friendship.

There was much smoking of peace pipes, Catlin said, but he never told how the white men felt about eating dog. He called the sacrifice of a dog a truly religious ceremony in which the Indians honored their guests. "I have seen an Indian take from the bowl the head of his dead animal, and talk of its affection and loyalty with tears in his eyes."

One day, preparing to paint Little Bear (*Mah-to-tchee-ga*), Catlin made a mistake that caused bloodshed. He would learn that this Indian's capacity for provoking insult was endless. Little Bear, a

Sioux Dog Feast. National Museum of American Art, Smithsonian Institution. Gift of Mrs. Joseph Harrison, Jr.

Hunkpapa, was looking off to one side and Catlin decided to paint him just as he stood. As usual there was an audience squatting and standing inside the studio teepee. The Dog (*Shon-ka*), a surly man of the Bad Arrow Points band, stood near the easel to get a better view. He was quiet for a few minutes, then, as Catlin wrote later, he said:

> *"Little Bear is but half a man."*
> *"Who says that?" Little Bear's voice had an edge to it.*
> *"The Dog says it."*

"Why does The Dog say it?"

"Ask the Medicine Painter. He knows you are but half a man, for he has painted but half your face."

"When The Dog says that, let him prove it. Little Bear can look at anyone, and now he is looking at an old woman and a coward!"

The Dog walked out and Little Bear resumed his position. He admired the finished portrait and gave Catlin a painted and decorated buckskin shirt. But his expression changed as he left, followed by the others who knew there would be a fight.

Little Bear went to his teepee for his muzzle-loading flintlock musket. He loaded it with powder and wad and dropped a lead ball down the barrel. Then he threw himself on the ground and asked the Great Spirit for help and protection. His wife saw how disturbed he was. She didn't know why he had loaded the gun, but was afraid for him and shook it until the lead ball dropped out.

Little Bear was still praying when the Dog's voice was heard outside, "If Little Bear is a whole man, let him come out and prove it!" Little Bear grabbed his gun and ran from the teepee, unaware that he was defenseless. The Dog fired and Little Bear fell, the side of his face shot away. The Hunkpapa warriors armed themselves, yelling their war cries. Warriors of both bands ran to their horses and open warfare broke out on the prairie. The Dog's arm was shattered by a musket ball. As the fighting continued, the women prepared to quickly break camp. The Hunkpapa warriors swore vengeance until the Dog was killed.

Catlin was suddenly the object of hatred. The Hunkpapas thought he had caused Little Bear's death—though his wife said she was responsible. It was one of the few times in the years Catlin spent among the Indians that his life was threatened. The

The Dog, Chief of the Bad Arrow Points Band. National Museum of American Art, Smithsonian Institution. Gift of Mrs. Joseph Harrison, Jr.

fur company people told him to pack and get aboard the *Yellowstone,* scheduled to depart early the next morning. But Catlin insisted on painting the breakup of the Sioux camp before he went on board.

He didn't learn the outcome of the feud until months later when he was returning east. He said there was "blood and butchery in the story." Little Bear's band pursued the Bad Arrow Points for many days. There were several battles, and Little Bear's brother was killed in one. His death and those of many others were also charged to Catlin. A solemn council was held—and he was condemned to death, along with the Dog. Only when he reached St. Louis did Catlin learn that the Dog had been tracked down and killed near the Black Hills. This ended the feud and the bands were once again friends.

Above Fort Pierre, the *Yellowstone* steamed past headlands and high sheer ridges that Catlin thought of as "some ancient and boundless city in ruins—ramparts, terraces, towers, citadels and castles—cupolas and magnificent porticoes, and here and there a solitary column and crumbling pedestal." Along the way he painted the strange, majestic landscape. The steamboat made few stops en route to Fort Union, eight hundred miles upriver. The high waters of early spring and summer would soon ebb and the *Yellowstone* might become stranded until the following year.

Catlin looked forward to one stop. Pigeon's Egg Head was returning to his Assiniboin village, a short distance below Fort Union. His military uniform was soiled now, the tall feather on his beaver hat broken and dangling over his face, the kid gloves almost black, his fan broken. But he still wore the sword and high-heeled boots, and had two bottles of whiskey in his pockets.

*He walked ashore with a keg of whiskey under his arm and blue
umbrella in one hand. He took position on the bank among his
relatives and friends. For a half-hour not one of them gave any sign of
recognition. He also gazed upon them . . . as if they were foreign to
him and he had nothing in common with them. Thus the mutual
gazing upon . . . when a gradual but cold and exceedingly formal
recognition began to take place. . . .*

The Assiniboin's end was tragic. He told tales of the white
man's cities and ways that defied Indian understanding. His people
marked him as a liar and imposter. He had been, they said, among
the white men, who are great liars and he had learned from them.
He sank into disgrace, but continued to strut around and lecture
on the manners and customs of the whites. The whiskey keg was
soon empty and he lost even his drinking friends. His uniform was
cut up for leggings and his wife's uses. All he had left was the
umbrella, which he kept open over his head night and day. On
buffalo hunts he did little more than preen and strut and tell tales
of what he had seen in the east. Within months he was killed by
his own people as a crazy, useless, no-good liar.

SEVEN

THE *YELLOWSTONE* STEAMED INTO FORT UNION ON JULY 17, 1832. It was located at the junction of the Missouri and Yellowstone rivers (the present North Dakota–Montana border). The fort was two hundred feet square and enclosed by a high stockade of cottonwood logs. The buildings comprised ten log cabins, storehouses, and sheds where fur was baled for shipment downriver. When Catlin arrived, large numbers of Blackfeet, Crow, Assiniboin, Cheyenne, and Cree were encamped there. Blackfeet and Crow were deadly enemies, as were Blackfeet and Assiniboin, Cheyenne and Crow. But the same conditions of truce held at every fort. The tribes mixed as friends—just waiting to leave and resume old hatreds.

Kenneth McKenzie ruled his wild empire like a medieval lord, the courageous, adventurous, and despotic "King of the Upper Missouri." Despite the location of the fort in unmapped, far distant country of the most warlike Indians, McKenzie lived in comfortable style:

He generally has some 40 to 50 men and 150 horses about him. His table groans under the luxuries of the country—with buffalo meat and tongues, beavers' tails, and marrow fat. . . . He has good wine. A bottle of Madeira and one of excellent Port are set in a pail of ice every day and finished at dinner.

McKenzie had vast stores of the usual trade goods and had added twenty thousand finger rings when he saw how Indians admired his own. There was little whiskey or rum, but he had forty barrels of pure alcohol. McKenzie and Chouteau schemed to beat the new government ban against shipping whiskey into Indian country. The American Fur Company was to secretly buy and ship a complete distillery to Fort Union.

McKenzie promised Catlin every opportunity to paint what he wanted. He was given private quarters, and a "studio" in a block-house on the wall of the fort.

My easel stands before me, and the cool breech of a cannon makes me a comfortable seat. . . . The operations of my brush are mysteries of the highest order to these red sons of the prairie. My room is full of wild and jealous spirits who all meet here to be amused and pay me honors. But they gaze upon each other with looks of deep-rooted hatred and revenge.

As each tribal chief was being painted, he felt it necessary to have Catlin guarded from other tribes. One day he was doing a portrait of the Blood chief Buffalo Bull's Back Fat (*Stee-mick-oh-suks*). While he posed, the chief was surrounded by his own warriors, but his Blackfoot and Piegan enemies also looked on. Catlin sensed the tension and danger in the studio:

Buffalo Bull's Back Fat, Head Chief, Blood Tribe. National Museum of American Art, Smithsonian Institution. Gift of Mrs. Joseph Harrison, Jr.

This is a curious scene, when one sits in the midst of such inflammable and bitter enemies. They are brought together unarmed in peace for the first time in their lives. Within a few weeks on the plains, the war cry will be raised against each other and their deadly bows will be drawn.

Catlin painted the head medicine man of the Blackfeet, the White Buffalo (*Wun-nes-tow*). A medicine man was the high priest, prophet, doctor, magician, and supernatural controller of human destiny. No other Indian, not a chief or the bravest warrior, had such influence over his people. "Medicine" played a vital role in primitive culture. Most Upper Missouri trappers were French, and the word comes from the French word for doctor, *medicin*.

To the Indian, "medicine" meant mystery or supernatural powers—not drugs. Each tribe, and bands within tribes, had their sacred medicine. It could be the hide of a white buffalo, a bearskin, eagle's beak, snakeskin, bat wing, racoon tail, or wolfskin. The sacred object was kept in a medicine bag, a "mystery bag," made of animal or reptile or bird skin, and stuffed with moss. Decorated according to a man's personal taste and beliefs, he prayed to it and looked to it for protection all his life.

When an Indian boy was about fourteen, he was said to be making or collecting his medicine. He went into the wilds for days and fasted. He lay on the ground and cried to the Great Spirit. When he fell asleep, the first creature he dreamed about was his medicine and he hunted it. The Indian carried his medicine bag into battle. If he lost it to an enemy, he suffered disgrace as great as if he sold it or gave it away. Until an Indian could capture a medicine bag from an enemy he'd killed, he was without honor in the tribe. But this done, the medicine was restored. When he died the medicine bag was buried with him—to take him to the beautiful hunting grounds in heaven. ("I have been unable to buy a medicine bag for my collection," wrote Catlin, "though I have offered extravagant prices.")

Catlin saw a medicine man performing his mysterious rites over a dying man. A party of Cree had come down from the north to make their summer camp and trade with the fur company. A big party of Blackfeet, enemies of the Cree, also came in to trade. Their business finished, the Cree started for their home country. One Cree, however, stayed behind and shot a Blackfoot chief. According to Catlin who witnessed the scene:

> *The Blackfoot fell and rolled around in the agonies of death. The Blackfeet chased the Crees who were riding fast for the northern bluffs. The fight lasted a half-hour or so and the Blackfeet returned to the fort. The medicine man approached the dying chief in a crouched position. His body and head were covered with the skin of a yellow bear, his own head inside that of the bear. The animal's huge claws hung from his wrist and ankles. In one hand he shook a rattle, in the other he brandished a medicine spear. He began jumping wildly, grunting, yelling, snarling and growling, dancing like a bear, and leaping around the wounded chief. This went on for an hour before the chief died.*

Of all the Indians he painted, Catlin most admired the Blackfeet and Crow. Both tribes were mounted civilizations of striking beauty and constant pageantry. They were the principal sources of trade for the fur company. Together, they ruled a broad sweep of the best beaver country westward into the Rocky Mountains.

The Blackfeet were an extremely hostile, warring tribe number-

Medicine Man, Performing His Mysteries over a Dying Man. National Museum of American Art, Smithsonian Institution. Gift of Mrs. Joseph Harrison, Jr.

ing about eighteen thousand. Only the Comanche could match their ferocity in battle. The Blackfeet were a marauding people, with fine strong bodies and richly clothed to reflect their prosperous culture. Although white men were just coming into their region, the Blackfeet were already defiant. They were willing to come to the fort to trade, but warned trappers to stay away from their domain. The fearless trappers ignored the warning, and each year some fifteen or twenty were killed by the Blackfeet. But they were no more hostile to whites than to their Indian enemies.

It was the Crow Catlin loved most, though. Thomas Farnham, an explorer, called them "the most thorough rascals, murder and robbery their principal employments." Prince Maximilian of Neuweid saw them in 1833 and said they were the proudest of Indians, and although they despised the whites, they did not kill them but often robbed them. Bernard De Voto wrote in *Across the Wide Missouri*: "Although the Crows fought all Indians, had bad morals and were thieves, they were friendly, and in many ways the most notable of all the Plains Indians."

The Crow were a smaller tribe than the Blackfeet, possibly seven thousand according to Catlin. No tribe equaled them in elegance of bearing and costume. No knight of old could match the virile beauty of a mounted Crow at the gallop, his lance streamers and shirt fringes fluttering, and his very long hair streaming out behind. Catlin described them as "handsome, with an ease and grace and dignity of manners . . . most of them six feet tall or more."

Catlin gloried in these tribes so little touched by white man's civilization:

They are all in a state of primitive wildness and are picturesque and fine-looking. . . . Of such tribes the Crows and Blackfeet stand first. No one can appreciate their nobility without seeing them in their own country. I will do all I can to make their looks and customs known to the world. I will paint and scribble, and bring their plumes, dresses, weapons, etc., and everything but the Indian himself to prove to the world what I have said.

He painted at incredible speed—everything and everybody: villages, hunts, dances, costumes, weapons, landscapes of the northwest prairie, warriors, women, and children. But his anxiety to paint as many Indians as possible made him return to the portraits so typical of his work. He resisted the temptation to generalize or type or romanticize his subjects. Every Indian was an individual to Catlin, and his skill in defining that quality was his true genius.

Catlin was very careful to document his paintings. He carried Certificates of Authentication that were signed on the spot by Indian agents, fur company people, army officers, anyone who had been a witness. A typical one read:

No. 131—Blackfoot, The Eagle Ribs (Pe-toh-pe-kiss). I hereby certify that this portrait was painted from life at Fort Union, mouth of the Yellowstone, in the year 1832, by George Catlin, and that the Indian sat in the costume in which it is painted.

John Sanford, United States Indian Agent

Catlin was fascinated by the dances of the Plains tribes, which reflected their very life. There were buffalo dances, scalp dances, sun dances, beggars' dances, rain and grass dances, and many oth-

Eagle's Ribs, a Piegan Chief. National Museum of American Art, Smithsonian
Institution. Gift of Mrs. Joseph Harrison, Jr.

Eagle Dance, Choctaw. National Museum of American Art, Smithsonian Institution. Gift of Mrs. Joseph Harrison, Jr.

ers. He was disturbed by the torture of the Sioux Sun Dance, but he watched without flinching so he could record it. The dance was a rite of initiation for young men, a test of bravery.

A medicine man gashed a dancer's chest and shoved sharpened sticks beneath the muscles. The sticks were attached to a rawhide rope hanging from a tall pole. The rope was pulled until the man was forced to stand on tiptoe, looking at the sun. His body was supported only by the sticks that tore into his flesh. If he endured, the dancer was cut down and given great honor and gifts. If he fell or fainted or cried out, he suffered disgrace all his life. Catlin thought he would never see anything worse, but he was to find a crueler ceremony among the Mandans.

The Buffalo Dance was vital to a hunting people. Dancers were chosen for their reputation as warriors and hunters. Vocal and instrumental music was an important part of the ritual. The dance steps were four kinds of basic foot-stamping. A dance to bring the buffalo or the rain were almost always successful—the Indians didn't stop dancing until it brought results.

The Beggars' Dance was an appeal to the Great Spirit to make the prosperous give to the poor. The Scalp Dance was equal in importance to the Buffalo Dance. It was usually in celebration of a victorious war party and often performed at night by torchlight. Victors returned with enemy scalps. Young women were chosen to hold the scalps while the warriors danced around them, jumping and stomping and yelling boasts of their bravery.

Catlin was a pioneer of American ethnography (the study of specific cultures). He witnessed customs and behavior among the Indians that he found barbaric and shocking. But he had the intelligence and understanding to learn what they meant in Indian life. He made no judgments and simply recorded what he saw.

When the Crow killed a buffalo cow, they sometimes raped it. They chopped joints off their fingers in mourning so often they hardly had a whole hand among them. The men saved their thumbs and a trigger finger. Crow men and women often made love in public in daylight.

Blackfeet chopped the noses off women who had committed adultery. A warrior might strip the skin off a dead enemy's body. They let each thumbnail grow until it curved like a claw.

The Comanche liked the curdled, partly digested milk in young buffalo calves. Assiniboin made a dish of buffalo blood boiled with brains, rosebuds, and hide scrapings. Arikara retrieved a drowned buffalo so putrified it could be eaten with a spoon. Many Indians ate fat young dogs and insects—and thought eating pork was disgusting.

Arikara practiced incest. Comanche enjoyed torturing prisoners. After a day of torturing, when they wanted relief from the prisoner's cries, they cut out his tongue. Indian children often lost an eye when they played with bows and arrows. For spiritual devotion, Cheyenne men stood up to their neck in water all day, or stood on a hill from sunrise to sunset, motionless except for turning their face to the sun.

Plains Indians showed no respect for the dead of their enemies. Many tribes buried their dead on scaffolds or in trees. Another tribe's war party might pull them down and trample the corpses with their horses. Catlin saw Blackfeet pull Assiniboin dead from a tree, kick the remains to pieces, then hold their rifles against the skulls and blow them to pieces.

EIGHT

CATLIN THOUGHT OF THE WEST AS A REFUGE FROM the vices of civilization—greed, business and political trickery, working for wages, the ugliness of rapidly growing eastern cities. To him, life on the Upper Missouri had virtue and beauty. The land, which seemed to stretch forever in a romantic haze, the Indian in the simplicity of nature, shut out that other world for him.

I can't say what degree of happiness these sons of nature attain in the world, and how that pleasure can be measured against those of civilized society. But I do not see that we gain much over them in our intellectual and commercial and refined pleasures. And judging from their happy faces, I would surely say their lives are much happier than ours.

Catlin began to get a vision of a great national park that would protect the Indian way of life, the buffalo, and other wildlife:

A National Park! *It would contain man and beast, in all the wild freshness of their native beauty! The world could see them in their pristine beauty for ages to come. . . . . I would ask no other monument to my memory than as the founder of such a haven!*

He meant nothing like the reservations that would degrade the Indians. It would be a vast land bordering on the Rocky Mountains where the Plains Indians and wildlife were preserved as in a time capsule. Today it seems like a naive, fruitless dream. But it was a measure of Catlin's devotion to the Indian cause—and his obsession to preserve their way of life. He soon realized that his paintings and writings would be the only record of that life.

In late July 1832 Catlin was ready to return to St. Louis. He had intended to paddle a canoe alone down the Missouri. But Kenneth McKenzie knew the dangers along the two-thousand-mile route. He insisted that Catlin take along two river men, Jean Ba'tiste, a French-Canadian, and Abraham Bogard, originally from Mississippi. They worked for the fur company transporting furs and supplies between remote stations in the wilderness. Now they were bound for St. Louis on leave to spend their pay in the saloons and brothels.

Before Catlin left, McKenzie took him into his own "museum" of Indian costumes and weapons and said to pick what he wanted. "I will send it on with the outfits of those fellows you painted. They will sell them for a drink or two when their throats get dry enough." He said Catlin would be glad to have two good marksmen along "when those damned Ricarees [Arikara] see you. They are about 200 miles past the Mandans and full of murder for whites. Keep in midstream through their country."

"We launched off one fine morning," Catlin wrote:

Our canoe was made of green timber and was heavy and awkward. But we were going with the current and were promised a fair and successful voyage. Ammunition was abundant, a good stock of buffalo tongues, beaver tails, and pemmican [an emergency ration of dried meat, berries, and fat pressed into small cakes]. *Thus fitted out, we swept off at a rapid rate under the shouts of the savages and cheers of our friends who lined the banks.*

The first days were pleasant and they made good progress. One night their camp was attacked by a grizzly and her cubs who chewed Catlin's precious paints and ate some of their food. But most of the days were an idyllic journey through a wilderness world that white men had rarely seen so close up.

Teeming herds of buffalo grazed along the river's edge and often blackened the green hills for miles beyond. Antelope, deer, and elk bounded by. Packs of gray wolves and an occasional grizzly roamed only yards away. Purple clouds built to the north. Cottonwood leaves showed their pale undersides in the wind. Whitecaps rose on the river and veils of dust blew down the buttes. They spotted mountain sheep on the sweep of cliffs. Cranes and geese and birds of every variety flew past.

They soon put in at Fort Clark, the fur company's trading post with the Mandan. The captain, James Kipp, had married into the tribe and guided Catlin and his companions to their village. As they approached, they were greeted by the howling and barking of hundreds of dogs running down to the river.

Catlin made paintings and observations of practically every phase of Mandan culture. He recorded their religious torture ceremony and other secret rites. The truth of his unusual pictures was doubted for a long time. Even after that truth was established, many experts couldn't believe such rituals were possible. His documentary evidence became even more important when the Mandan were wiped out in the smallpox epidemic of 1837. In 1885, Thomas Donaldson of the Smithsonian Institution wrote: "If Mr. Catlin had visited no other Indian tribe but the Mandan, his notes and paintings of these Indians would alone preserve his memory."

The Mandan were a small tribe of about two thousand who called themselves People of the Pheasants. They lived in two permanent villages two miles apart. The tribe so intrigued Catlin that over half of his first volume of *Letters and Notes on the Manners, Customs, and Conditions of the North American Indians* was devoted to the Mandan. "So forcibly have I been struck by the peculiar ease and elegance of these people, I am fully convinced that they have sprung from some other origin than that of other North American Indians." Many Mandans had fair complexions, soft hair, blue or gray or hazel eyes, and light-colored or gray hair. They were a fine-looking people, erect, supple, and graceful.

They lived in lodges forty to sixty feet in diameter. These were made of timbers with earth packed solidly around the outside. Their villages were built on banks forty feet above the river and had only the backside to protect with an eighteen-foot wood stockade. With powerful foes, and because they were a small tribe, they trained from childhood to defend their fortress. They were hunter-farmers, but their lives were much like those of city-dwellers. On sunny days tribal life centered on the domed roofs of their lodges. Catlin once climbed to a roof and told what he saw:

Groups standing or reclining . . . groups engaged in games . . . women making robes or dresses . . . others asleep or merely basking in the hot sun . . . laughing children and dogs . . . buffalo skulls, drying

73

Bird's-Eye View of the Mandan River, 1800 Miles above St. Louis. National Museum of American Art, Smithsonian Institution. Gift of Mrs. Joseph Harrison, Jr.

skins, their strange round bullboats, pottery, snowshoes, and other articles. . . .

He admired the Mandan women's beauty, cleanliness, and richness of dress. It was the only tribe where he might have been tempted to break his marriage vows. "A beautiful girl is worth only perhaps two horses, a gun with powder and ball for a year, five pounds of beads, or a couple of gallons of whiskey." He was drawn to a lovely young woman named the Mink (*Mi-neek-e-sunk-te-ka*). But in the end he resisted. She would only be a burden on his journey, and he was too moral to "marry" her and leave her behind.

Mint, a Pretty Girl. National Museum of American Art, Smithsonian Institution. Gift of Mrs. Joseph Harrison, Jr.

The Mandan were extremely intelligent, showed talent in music and art, and were more advanced in their crafts than most tribes. They spent far less time in warfare than in pleasures. Mandan men loved feasting, personal display, and talking about their conquests. A warrior took a steambath, plunged into the cold river, then hurried home wrapped in a buffalo robe to have his wife rub him with bear grease. He had a pleasant nap, and afterward he dressed in his finest clothes for a social visit, a feast or dance, or just to parade around the village. But nothing absorbed the Mandan as deeply as their legends of the past. These were part of the religious rites that Catlin painted and said were "hard to believe if not seen."

Catlin became good friends with Four Bears (*Mah-to-toh-pa*), a valiant chief. He described him as "the most extraordinary man . . . wearing a robe with the history of his battles upon it." The chief invited Catlin to his lodge for a feast of buffalo roast and pudding of wild turnips and currants. Four Bears cut a slice from the roast and threw it into the fire as a sacrifice. He then signaled Catlin to begin—a Plains chief never ate with his honored guests, but served them. When Catlin finished eating, Four Bears filled a pipe with *knick-kneck*. It was a mixture of tobacco, red willow bark, and shavings of castor (an oily substance from a beaver gland). The mixture might be dusted with powdered buffalo dung as tinder for easy lighting. The two friends settled themselves to smoke "in the most delightful exchange of good feelings and pantomime gestures."

Through Kipp's influence, Catlin was allowed to enter the Mandan's most sacred circle and the dark temple of tortures. He and Kipp were the first white men to see *O-kee-pa,* the Mandan

Four Bears, Second Chief, in Full Dress. National Museum of American Art, Smithsonian Institution. Gift of Mrs. Joseph Harrison, Jr.

torture ceremony—and Catlin was the only man to paint it. In a few years the Mandan were gone.

No ritual of primitive people anywhere was as excruciatingly painful as this self-imposed torture. Sacrifice was important in Plains Indian religion. It could take many forms—the simple offering of meat cast into the fire, burning the first ear of corn before the harvest, chopping a finger off, killing a favorite horse or dog, or pain that brought a man near death. But nothing equaled the ordeal of *O-kee-pa.*

Catlin was told it had three purposes: to celebrate the subsiding of an ancient flood; to make the buffalo herds fertile; and to allow young braves to prove their manhood and endurance.

The ceremonies began with a naked man, painted white, arriving from the prairie. He wore a headdress of raven skins and carried a large pipe. The next morning at sunrise he entered the "medicine lodge," followed by many young men who would endure the torture. For the next three days they fasted and prayed, while other men performed the Bull Dance. A yelling devil-man, painted black, suddenly dashed into the crowd of screaming women ringing the dancers. The women chased him back to the prairie, and then the tortures began as eerie music played.

Sharp sticks were hooked through deep cuts in each man's breast, shoulders, and thighs. His shield, bow and quiver, and heavy buffalo skulls were hung on the sticks. Ropes were lowered from the top of the lodge and fastened to the sticks. He was raised, blood streaming, until his feet were about eight feet off the ground. When completely suspended, he was turned with a pole, gently at first, then faster and faster until he couldn't stand the agony and cried out to the Great Spirit to make him brave.

As a victim dropped the medicine bag he was holding, he was

lowered and left on the ground, almost lifeless. No one was allowed to help him. When he came to and had enough strength, he staggered or crawled to a tribal elder who then chopped off the man's little finger as a further sacrifice.

After a group of braves had been mutilated this way, they were led out to the Big Canoe, a large wooden barrellike structure. Rawhide thongs were tied around their wrists. Two men grabbed each victim by the thongs and raced him around the Big Canoe. If he fell, he was dragged until the weight of the shield or bow and quiver or buffalo skull pulled the sharp sticks from his flesh. This ended the ordeal.

Each man lay where he fell until he could rise without help. Then, staggering and bleeding, he would make his way through the crowd to his own lodge. Family, relatives, and friends would welcome him with admiration rather than sympathy—for now he was a full-fledged Mandan.

Catlin painted four scenes of the terrible rites. Suffering from a fever, excited, he made them with slashes and splashes of color, crowding the canvas with grotesque monsters and maniacs. They create an impression of savage wildness and action that is unforgettable.

Catlin left the Mandan with great regret. His canoe was in the middle of the river, the village receding into a point of firelight in the distance, when he suddenly heard startling yells. A group of Indians was running along the shore, hailing him. The trappers paddled to shore and Catlin was told the Mink was dying. The painting Catlin had made of her, they said, was too much like her . . . when the canoe left the village Catlin was taking part of her life with it. She was bleeding from the mouth—"You are drawing the strings out of her heart and they will soon break. We must

Bull Dance, Mandan O-Kee-Pa Ceremony.
National Museum of American Art,
Smithsonian Institution. Gift of Mrs.
Joseph Harrison, Jr.

take her picture back and then she will be well again." Catlin unrolled his bundle of portraits. Reluctant to part with it, he gave it to the Indians and wished her well. Later he discovered that she had died—and he was thought to have caused it.

Catlin didn't learn of the destruction of the Mandan by smallpox until 1838, when James Kipp visited him in New York. The disease spread like wildfire through their villages and only thirty or forty survived. They became slaves of the Arikara. Some months later, the Arikara were attacked by a Sioux war party. The Mandan ran out and called to the Sioux to kill them: "Our people are all dead and we do not wish to live!" The Sioux obliged and slaughtered them all.

NINE

CATLIN AND THE TWO TRADERS HAD ENJOYED THEIR
passage downriver so far, but they were now in the country of the
dreaded Arikara. The tribe had sworn terrible death to every
white man who fell into their hands.

As it grew dark they saw the smoke of an Arikara village ahead.
They took the canoe closer to shore and lay under some willows.
They heard the yelps and war cries of the people known as the
"horrid tribe." The moon rose full and bright, and they stayed
hidden for a while. But Catlin remembered McKenzie's advice
about staying in the middle of the river. Covered by brush, they
pushed out into the current.

As they drifted past the village, they saw "a scene of thrilling
nature. A hundred torches were swung about, and some fresh
scalps hung on the poles . . . in the nightly ceremony of frightful
shrieks and yells and gestures of the scalp dance. . . . After I got
some hundred miles below, I learned that they were dancing with
two white men's scalps taken in revenge against the traders."

Once they were caught in the middle of a great buffalo herd
swimming across the Missouri on their southward migration. The

three men had heard the drumming of the herd when they were still miles off. When the buffalo came in sight, the river was black with their horned heads as they fought to reach the opposite bank. Ba'tiste and Bogard maneuvered the canoe safely to shore and they waited until the herd had crossed.

They moved downriver through what is now South Dakota, Nebraska, Kansas, and Missouri, stopping at villages along the way. Catlin painted a number of tribes but liked the Pawnee best. He did a strong portrait of a Grand Pawnee chief, the Horse Chief (*Shon-ka-ki-he-ga*). They were a formidable, brainy people who ranged wide across the plains. A match in battle for any enemy, they were also expert thieves, liars, and extortioners. Their country lay square in the path of an advancing white empire, and later they became outstanding scouts for the U.S. Army.

The first cool winds made Catlin and his companions hurry on to St. Louis. The small craft was loaded with paintings, sketchbooks, and notebooks. Getting them back safely was only the first step in the fulfillment of Catlin's dream. Ragged, bearded, and grimy, the travelers finally paddled the canoe among the big river steamboats at anchor in the port of St. Louis.

John C. Ewers of the Smithsonian, an authority on the art of the West, estimated the enormity of Catlin's work:

From the first day among the Sioux at Fort Pierre, Catlin spent eighty-six days traveling. He painted 135 pictures, collected Indian artifacts, and wrote many pages of valuable notes. The paintings included 66 Indians painted from life, 36 scenes of Indian life, 25 landscapes, and at least 8 hunting scenes. 'Only a man of boundless energy, roused to a feverish pitch of creativity, could have performed all these tasks in so short a period.'

Horse Chief, Grand Pawnee Head Chief. National Museum of American Art, Smithsonian Institution. Gift of Mrs. Joseph Harrison, Jr.

In *The Natural Man Observed: A Study of Catlin's Indian Gallery,* William H. Truettner of the Smithsonian estimates Catlin's production at 170 paintings. Catlin, he says, "took no more than a brief likeness in the field, and the buffalo hunts and scenes of Indian life were probably studio productions of the following winter and spring."

Catlin heard that the leaders of the Black Hawk War were imprisoned in Jefferson Barracks, ten miles from St. Louis. He got permission to visit and was heartsick when he saw Black Hawk, the Sauk and Fox chief, his two sons, and many others in chains. He painted some of the still-defiant prisoners. One, the Soup (*Nah-pope*), grabbed the ball and chain fastened to his leg, raised it and shouted, "Make me so, and show me to the White Father!" When Catlin refused to paint him in that pose, the Soup kept changing his position and grimacing so Catlin couldn't catch a true likeness.

He stayed in St. Louis for a time and worked on his paintings. In late December he headed east to be with his wife. They met in Pittsburgh, Pennsylvania. By then his lungs were inflamed and he was very sick for a month. He didn't go west in 1833. Instead, he decided to take a year off to finish the previous season's fieldwork. Catlin, however, was too restless to stay in a studio and he was anxious to make money to pay for the next expedition.

He opened an exhibit of his paintings in Pittsburgh in April 1833. The *Pittsburgh Gazette* reported: "The total number which he began during his expedition is very large. Most of them are in an unfinished state, he only having had sufficient leisure to secure correct likenesses." Catlin overheard people's comments—"uncouth" . . . "crude" . . . "bunkum"—and was discouraged. Clara saved the day by insisting that he talk to the audience about the Indians.

He next took the paintings to Cincinnati, Ohio. Judge James Hall, editor of *Western Monthly Magazine,* was enthusiastic: "A collection of the most extraordinary and interesting paintings that we have ever witnessed. One which constitutes a most valuable addition to the history of our continent, as well as to the arts of our country." The exhibition moved on to Louisville, Kentucky, toward the end of the year, and again it was successful.

Black Rock, a Two Kettle (?) Chief. National Museum of American Art, Smithsonian Institution. Gift of Mrs. Joseph Harrison, Jr.

Judge Hall had seen the truth that Catlin wanted to bring to the public. "These are not portraits of the depraved savages who linger upon the edge of our advanced settlements. They are those of the manly Indian, as he exists on his own wide plains, joint tenant with the buffalo, elk and grizzly bear, and they exhibit in a striking manner the distinctive features of the tribes to which they belong." Some years later Judge Hall and Thomas McKenney published *The Indian Tribes of North America.* They had wanted to illustrate it with Catlin's paintings, but by that time he had publishing plans of his own.

Catlin and his wife sailed down the Ohio and Mississippi rivers for New Orleans, Louisiana, from Cincinnati, then around the coast to Pensacola, Florida, where they spent the winter with his younger brother James, a banker. In March and April, they were back in New Orleans, where he lectured and exhibited his collection to enthusiastic audiences.

In the spring of 1834 he was off on an adventure that would take him deep into the country of the fierce Comanche, called the "Lords of the South Plains." Again, Clara was left alone. She returned to St. Louis from New Orleans by steamboat, then by stagecoach to Alton, Illinois, where she stayed with friends until his return in the fall.

Secretary of War Lewis Cass granted Catlin permission to accompany the First Regiment of Mounted Dragoons on a military expedition. Their mission was to ride southwest and contact the predatory Comanche, Pawnee, and Wichita tribes. The regiment, mostly seasoned veterans, was newly formed at Jefferson Barracks. Among them was Lieutenant Jefferson Davis, a veteran of the Black Hawk War. He had observed Catlin painting the prisoners, and later would figure large at a crucial point in Catlin's life.

Catlin was to meet the regiment at Fort Gibson, a remote outpost far up the Arkansas River (present Oklahoma). His dead brother Julius had served there, and he suffered some of the old guilt as he came through the gate. Waiting for the regiment to arrive, Catlin painted the Five Civilized Tribes—Cherokee, Creek, Choctaw, Chickasaw, and Seminole—forced from their southeastern land by the Indian Removal Act. Catlin hired a man named Joe Chadwick to accompany him, and they gathered supplies and horses for the trip farther west. He wrote that he "purchased the finest horse in that country for $250 and named him 'Charley,' a mustang of cream color with black tail and mane. He was broken by Comanche Indians."

The dragoons commanded by Colonel Henry Dodge finally arrived, then rode out of Fort Gibson six days later on June 19, 1834, bugles blowing and guidons fluttering. "The regiment makes a striking picture," wrote Catlin. "Each company has a different-colored horse. There are bays, blacks, whites, creams, palominos and sorrels. . . . We start today for Comanche country, and God only knows where that is." He and Chadwick rode at the head of the column with Colonel Dodge and General Henry Leavenworth. The general, who planned the expedition, was to ride with the regiment only as far as the Red River, about two hundred miles. Although it was originally intended to be a 715-man force, only 455 men actually rode out.

The regiment pressed forward at a fast pace to make up for a delayed start. Catlin marveled at the lush and striking landscape as the column rode southwest. They crossed high bluffs that offered a sweeping view of the horizon, then "trailed through broad and verdant valleys choked with vegetation." Often they found their progress "completely stopped by hundreds of acres of small plum trees closely interwoven and interlocked, and amongst these were beds of wild roses and wild currants, and gooseberries . . . and about them huge masses of prickly pears, and beautiful and tempting wildflowers that sweetened the air."

Nearing the Red River, men began to fall sick with a bilious fever that affected the liver and gall bladder. It was probably caused by a combination of blazing summer heat on the unshaded plains, contaminated food, and foul water. It quickly grew into an epidemic and many men and horses were close to death. General Leavenworth, very sick himself, ordered Dodge to continue the march with any men fit to ride. Catlin and Chadwick went with them.

The sun was merciless and there was little drinkable water. More men came down with the fever. In a few days, less than half of those who rode out of the Red River camp could still sit in a saddle. The regimental report stated on July 18: "Six litters of sick, including Mr. Catlin." Day after day Colonel Dodge led his dragoons westward. For a time they had fresh buffalo meat, and there were enough men to tend the sick.

Indian scouts signaled back that they were finding fresh tracks of Comanche horsemen. Dodge was aware that the Comanches knew of their presence, teasing them deeper and deeper into their country. He was no longer sure his troop would be received peaceably. Any good-sized war party could destroy them to the last man.

One day at noon a large party of horsemen were spotted on a distant ridge. Their lances glistened in the sun and at first it was thought to be Mexican cavalry. But as the horsemen drew closer, an officer, scanning with a spyglass, made out a party of Comanche. Dodge gave the order to advance slowly, in a skirmish

Wa-ho-beck-ee, a Handsome Brave. National Museum of American Art, Smithsonian Institution. Gift of Mrs. Joseph Harrison, Jr.

line, toward them. The Comanche suddenly disappeared and soon showed themselves on a far-off ridge. The regiment swung toward them, then Dodge called a halt. Showing the white flag, he rode out with a few officers. Catlin somehow found enough strength to mount his horse.

> *I joined in the advance, and the Indians stood their ground until we had come within a half-mile of them . . . at which one of their party galloped out in advance of the war party on a milk-white horse, carrying a piece of white buffalo skin on the point of his long lance.*

Catlin said it was the start of one of the most thrilling and beautiful scenes he ever witnessed. The Comanche leader approached, reining and spurring his horse, tacking left and right. He came close, leaned his lance against the flag, then wheeled and pranced up to Colonel Dodge. His hand was extended and Dodge quickly grapsed it. Everyone shook his hand. His party galloped forward and each warrior rode out along the ranks and shook every trooper's hand. When Catlin painted the Comanche leader, he learned that his name was the Little Spaniard (*His-oo-san-chess*). He was half-Spanish. The Comanche usually had contempt for half-breeds, but this man was one of the great leaders and warriors of the entire nation.

The Little Spaniard invited them to their village at the base of the Wichita Mountains. The dragoons were astonished at its size, about eight hundred teepees and thousands of superb horses. The Comanche gave demonstrations of their acrobatic riding skill in a sham battle—slipping off the side of a horse to shoot arrows from under its neck, or even shooting from below the animal's belly. Cavalry officers stationed at frontier posts in later years said the

Little Spaniard. National Museum of American Art, Smithsonian Institution. Gift of Mrs. Joseph Harrison, Jr.

Thighs, a Wichita Woman. National Museum of American Art, Smithsonian Institution. Gift of Mrs. Joseph Harrison, Jr.

Comanche were the greatest cavalry in the world. Catlin once thought that no tribe was as skilled on horse as the Crow, but the Comanche were even better.

He noted that Comanche men were hard-faced, short, and bowlegged. They were awkward on foot but "in riding they are not equalled by any other Indian on the continent."

The Colt repeating revolver was developed to fight the Comanche. Its rapid firing made it the perfect weapon against an enemy who could ride and shoot arrows with incredible speed and skill. The first time the Texas Rangers used the Colt in battle with the Comanche was the first time they won.

Catlin began painting Comanche and the visiting Kiowa and Waco. But he became so sick he couldn't ride on to the Pawnee Pict and Wichita villages with the dragoons. He lay weak with fever in the Comanche village until the regiment returned. Some of his portraits of Comanche tribal leaders may have been painted later at Fort Gibson while he recovered. A favorite subject was a chief he said was "the fattest and largest Indian I ever saw," the Mountain of Rocks (*Ta-wah-que-nah*).

Accompanied by the leading chiefs of the Comanche, Kiowa, and Wichita, the regiment marched back to Fort Gibson in less than three weeks along a northern route. Catlin, at times delirious with fever, had to be carried in a baggage wagon. The expedition had taken two months, and 151 of the original 455 men had died. But they accomplished their mission—making the first contact with the little-known, powerful tribes of the southern plains.

Catlin made plans to return to his wife in Alton, Illinois. He decided to ride "Charley," his horse, all the way to St. Louis. Everyone at the fort tried to discourage him, telling him he was far too weak, but he wouldn't change his mind. It was another test of his remarkable endurance. He had to ride across corners of Oklahoma and Arkansas and across Missouri to St. Louis, some five hundred lonely and dangerous miles.

I was feeble, but every hour gaining strength. When I felt a chill and the fever coming on, I dismounted and lay on the grass until I felt able

95

to continue. Every night I managed to bivouac on the bank of some stream or river, with water to make coffee and wood to make a fire. . . . My health improved daily.

Catlin crossed the rain-swollen Osage River by building a raft to hold his clothes, saddle, and paintings, which were in a metal tube. He drove the horse across while pushing the raft. At Booneville he ferried over the Missouri River to Alton on the east bank, and joined Clara. "There under the roof of some kind and hospitable friends, I found my dear wife, who had patiently waited to receive me back, a wreck."

They again spent the winter in New Orleans and Florida. Catlin did landscapes and worked on the Southwestern paintings. But most of the time he seemed content to indulge in "recreations and amusements" and be close to his wife. She sensed, however, that he would soon be anxious to go west again, but knew he was still too weak. She also was worried about the black moods he suffered. She timidly suggested that they just relax that summer, and to her great surprise, Catlin agreed. He planned what he called "a fashionable tour" up the Mississippi to the Falls of St. Anthony in Minnesota. "Like a wild bird of passage I started at the rallying cry of the wild goose for the fresh coolness of the north."

But Catlin's restlessness—his obsession to learn the Indians' secrets—turned it into another adventure.

T E N

THE CATLINS CELEBRATED THE FOURTH OF JULY 1835 at Fort Snelling, nine miles below the Falls, "in the presence of several hundred Chippewas [Ojibways] and as many hundreds of Sioux." The region was the eastern edge of the Sioux domain. Although the trip was supposed to be a vacation, Catlin had taken his art materials. He painted the Yankton Sioux and Chippewa, but they were hardly the primitives he loved:

> They are poor and meanly clad compared to those tribes on the Missouri . . . their morals and constitutions have deteriorated because they live close to white men in the vicinity of settlements, where they are sold whiskey and the small pox and other diseases are introduced.

While at Fort Snelling he learned about the fabled Pipestone Quarry from Black Dog, a Yankton Sioux chief, and Blue Medicine, a medicine man, while they sat for portraits. The quarry was the only source of the soft red stone from which Indian tribes throughout North America made their smoking pipes. It was extremely sacred ground—no white man had ever been permitted to set foot there. Black Dog and Blue Medicine were friendly, but Catlin knew it was their religious duty to keep white men out of the holy area. He realized they would kill any intruder, but that didn't stop him. He was determined to find the quarry at the first opportunity.

The Catlins began their voyage downriver separately. "I placed my wife on board the steamer, with a party of ladies, for Prairie du Chien [present Wisconsin]." Catlin bought a light and swift birchbark canoe from the Chippewa and "embarked on my homeward course." A few miles downriver, some drunken Yankton Sioux shot at his canoe. Catlin quickly paddled to shore and was met by yelling, laughing Indians. "Thrusting pistols in my belt, and with my double-barreled gun, I leaped ashore. I quickly slipped sketchbook and pencil into my hand, and under my gun each fellow stood for his likeness. . . . Some allowance must be made for their outrage. For many years they have been made drunkards by white men, and are often disposed to return insult for their injuries."

Several weeks later he rejoined Clara at Prairie du Chien, where he painted Winnebago and Menominee. He put Clara on a steamboat for Dubuque, Iowa, and continued his canoe voyage "happily alone, cooking my own food and having my own fun as I paddled along." At Dubuque, he and Clara sailed on the first southbound boat to Camp Des Moines, Iowa, where she took a steamer to St. Louis. He went overland to a Sauk and Fox village where he painted the Running Fox (*Kee-o-kuk*), who had become chief after Black Hawk's capture.

He met the always patient and uncomplaining Clara in St. Louis and they went east to visit their families. Clara was expecting their first child and she returned to Albany in January 1836. Catlin went to Pittsburgh to prepare an exhibit of his paintings. The foul air of the city, he claimed, would tone down the colors to a more "realistic tint." In late spring his collection was shipped to Buffalo for a grand opening in early July of that year.

Plans were changed when Clara lost the child. He immediately canceled the exhibition, and the family assumed it was the act of a devoted husband. But the death of the child gave Catlin another chance to go west. The tragedy, for him, was a chance to search for the legendary Pipestone Quarry. His father spoke harshly to him, but Clara understood his urgency. She knew he loved her and was crushed by the loss of the child. She understood his fear that the primitive Indian life would vanish before he could finish his work.

The smoking of the peace pipe was common to all North American tribes. It was an ancient ritual with religious meaning. Pipes were made in different shapes, but the bowls were all made from the same reddish stone. Each tribe, or band of a tribe, had its own variation of a belief that went back deep into their past. The Great Spirit had spoken to the people at the site of the red pipestone, saying it was a sacred meeting place of peace for all tribes. Indians believed that if a white man went there, it would offend the Great Spirit and he would punish them.

Catlin had heard all the stories and was certain he would be in great danger—no matter the friendliness of Indians in the past. It made no difference to him. Danger had always quickened his pulse.

The quarry was located at the Couteau Des Parieries, west of Fort Snelling. He left on a Great Lakes steamer, with stops at Detroit and Sault Sainte Marie, Michigan, and Green Bay, Wisconsin. By August 1836 he had canoed down the Fox and Wisconsin rivers to Prairie du Chien with Robert Serill Wood, an Englishman. They continued to the mouth of the Minnesota River, then changed to horses for the overland journey to the quarry. About 150 miles from their destination, they stopped at a small trading post.

A large party of angry Sioux was at the post and they crowded around the two men, threatening them if they continued on. They said they knew where the white men were going—to find out how much the land at the Pipestone Quarry was worth and take it from them. They would never surrender the land to white men.

Catlin spoke to them through Le Blanc, the trader. "We are merely two poor men traveling to see the Sioux and shake their hands, and examine what is interesting in their country." A young warrior pushed up close, his face inches from Catlin's. He saw the hatred in the Indian's eyes and was afraid he might suddenly pull his scalping knife. Le Blanc said the Sioux meant business and they should go back. But Catlin casually told him, "We have started to go and see it, and we cannot think of being stopped."

At every village and trading post, they were told to go back, but they persisted. They reached the forbidden place, deep in Sioux country, in the southwestern corner of Minnesota. At the crest of a long bare ridge, they found the sacred quarry.

The most striking feature of the place was a sheer thirty-foot wall of "close-grained, compact quartz, and extending for two miles where it disappears at both ends into the prairie. . . . It is stratified in several layers from pale grayish-red to dark blood-red. When freshly quarried it is soft enough to be carved in any desired shape with stone knives."

Catlin felt that he had come closer than ever before in understanding the secret heart of the Indians. "I am encamped on the

Pipestone Quarry. National Museum of American Art, Smithsonian Institution. Gift of Mrs. Joseph Harrison, Jr.

very rock where the Great Spirit stood when he consecrated the *pipe of peace* and smoked it to the tribes assembled around him. . . . Not far from us is the deep impression of the footsteps of the Great Spirit, in the form of a large bird. It is where he stood when the blood of buffalos that he was devouring ran into the rocks and turned them red."

He spent several days at the quarry, sketching and collecting samples of the stone. Later, he sent samples for analysis by Dr. Charles T. Jackson, a noted Boston mineralogist. Jackson said it was a new mineral, and named it Catlinite in his honor.

On his way home Catlin witnessed a treaty signing. The Sauk and Fox tribe was selling land to the U.S. government, represented by Colonel Henry Dodge, now Superintendent of Indians Affairs for the Wisconsin Territory. After the signing, the Indians

Keokuk on Horseback. National Museum of American Art, Smithsonian Institution. Gift of Mrs. Joseph Harrison, Jr.

were told to move their families and horses from the two hundred fifty thousand acres they just sold for $75 an acre. The Running Fox, now the head chief, laughed and said, "Father, we have left the lands already and sold our teepees to the Chemokemons [white men], some for one hundred and some for two hundred dollars. There are already four hundred Chemokemons moving in. Three days ago, one sold his teepee to another for two thousand dollars, to build a great town."

Catlin was amused, but regretted that Indians were quickly taking to the white man's sharp business practice. Then he realized that it was inevitable, and decided that Indians swindling white men for a change was a good thing. He asked the Running Fox if he had ever seen the Pipestone Quarry. The chief said, "No, I have never seen it. It is in our enemy's country. I wish it was in ours. I would sell it to the whites for a great many boxes of money."

Catlin's steamboat arrived in St. Louis late at night and he went to a hotel. He left his canoe on deck, his paintings and a bundle of Indian materials in his stateroom. Returning in the morning, he discovered that the canoe, some paintings, and materials were stolen. "This explained the losses I had met with before, losing boxes and parcels I sent back to St. Louis by steamer. What a comment this is upon the glorious advantages of civilization." Gathering what was left, he went off to Albany.

Catlin had no idea he had painted his last pictures of Indians west of the Mississippi. He had made a pictorial and written record of the principal tribes of the vast American West. His collection of tribal costumes, weapons, and other artifacts was the finest ever assembled. It was as unique as it was wide-ranging. He was certain the collection of paintings and materials would become the nucleus of a great national museum sponsored by the government.

Now he was ready to show his treasures to the world. He wanted people to know the true character of western Indians, and work for their cause. He hoped to promote his idea of a great national park along the edge of the Rocky Mountains, a permanent sanctuary for Indians and game animals of the West. He also planned to write a book.

He wanted to open his first exhibition in New York City. But he wrote his brother Francis that he wanted his pictures "more completed" and was "too poor to do anything." It was hardly surprising after six years of supporting himself by an occasional portrait commission and selling a few copies of his Indian subjects. He seemed to have survived those years by spending almost nothing, except for his 1833 exhibition tour. Otherwise, he begged passage for his Indian travels, spent winters with relatives, and left Clara with her wealthy family. For her sake, they probably helped when the Catlins needed money.

His exhibition had two trial runs in Albany and nearby Troy. Confident, he opened in New York at Clinton Hall on September 25, 1837. The catalog, a tribute to his labors, listed:

311 portraits of 45 tribes, 82 landscapes, 17 sporting scenes, 39 amusements, 28 manners and customs, 4 Mandan religious ceremonies.

A Crow tipi, Indian cradle, Comanche lances, peace-pipes, men's and women's dresses decorated with scalplocks of their enemies, War Eagle and Raven headdresses, necklaces.

Bows, arrows, quivers, shields, spears, war clubs, knives, tomahawks, Buffalo robes, belts, wampum, whistles, rattles, drums, etc. etc. etc.

The exhibition was a great success. Audiences were enthusiastic, astonished and full of praise. But there was also confusion, disbelief, even hostility. The West and its inhabitants were a mystery to people in the East. There had been almost no paintings of the Indians and the region. Most writing was at best highly imaginative, at worst false and damaging.

Catlin was presenting, for the first time, a true account of a people and landscape that had a powerful influence on the popular imagination. Many people, however, found it hard to believe that this smallish, mild-mannered artist could have wandered alone among so many tribes without being scalped or tortured. They thought his account of the Mandan torture ceremony "claptrap" and "blustiferation."

Most Americans saw the Indians only as one of two stereotypes— a noble warrior or a dirty, bloodthirsty savage. Catlin was trying to show that they were more human and complex than that. He said they had a culture of their own, and it was as worthy as any civilization east of the Mississippi. He warned that greedy, bigoted, unscrupulous white men were destroying that culture.

He spoke strongly against Indian agents who ruled like kings over great areas of the West, peddling cheap whiskey, debauching the Indian character, teaching them by example to cheat and steal and be immoral—and building hatred for all white people. He was also too frank about the government's poor record in keeping the promises made in land treaties with the Indians.

It is astonishing that under all the invasions, force, frauds and deceptions practiced on the Indians to push them from their lands, these abused people have exercised so little cruelty as they have. . . . I can say that the North American Indian—in his native state—is honest, hospitable, faithful, warlike, cruel, relentless—and an honorable and religious human being.

Steep Wind, a Brave of the Bad Arrow Points Band. National Museum of American Art, Smithsonian Institution. Gift of Mrs. Joseph Harrison, Jr.

In November the Running Fox and twenty of his tribe came to New York City, and Catlin invited them to the exhibition. When their appearance was publicized, almost two thousand people came even though the admission was doubled to one dollar. When Catlin showed the painting of the Running Fox on horseback, all the Indians suddenly sprang to their feet with yells and cries. The audience shrank back in fear, but the chief calmed his people. He told the audience they were excited seeing him on his favorite war horse, which "they all recognized." It was the first time Catlin had live Indians to confirm his lectures. After that, if possible, he always had Plains tribesmen wherever he exhibited.

Catlin was now making another kind of history—presenting the first Wild West show for the entertainment of the public. It was that subtle switch from artist, explorer, and ethnographer to showman and promoter that would bring sadness and ruin to his life.

ELEVEN

CATLIN CLOSED HIS EXHIBITION IN LATE DECEMBER, just as his first daughter, Elizabeth, was born. He had learned that Osceola (the Black Drink) and his warriors were imprisoned at Fort Moultrie, South Carolina, at the close of the Seminole War. They had been among the last to resist removal to the West. Catlin rushed south and discovered that Osceola's capture proved the government's treachery. The old chief had been captured— not in battle—but at a "peace conference" under a flag of truce.

Osceola posed for Catlin, who was told by the post doctor that the chief was very sick and would die soon. "This gallant fellow," he wrote, "is grieving with a broken spirit, and ready to die cursing the white man." He stayed at the fort until January 29, 1838, then left for New York. Osceola died the next day. The chief and other Seminoles were the last Indians he would paint while in the United States.

Catlin opened a new exhibition at Stuyvesant Institute in New York. He intended to use Osceola to call attention to the government's harsh Indian policy. But he was also aware that the Seminole portraits would make his collection more valuable. A full-

Osceola, the Black Drink, a Warrior of Great Distinction. National Museum of American Art, Smithsonian Institution. Gift of Mrs. Joseph Harrison, Jr.

length print of Osceola sold very well during the exhibition. The time seemed right to press Washington to buy the collection.

He had begun his campaign a year earlier. Purchase of the Indian Gallery had been debated in the 1837–1838 session of

Congress. Catlin's personality, talent, and purpose brought him many admirers in Washington. Daniel Webster, Henry Clay, William Seward, and other powerful senators fought for him. On April 9, 1838, Catlin opened an exhibition in Washington at the Old Theater. Even then, Washington was a city of rumor, and Catlin heard that the government would offer $150,000 for the Indian Gallery. But in the end there was no offer from Congress. Some "insiders" said the sale didn't happen because the government had a guilty conscience about its treatment of the Indian—and Catlin had too strongly reminded everyone of it.

Catlin was discouraged, but never wavered. He took the collection on tour for the summer and fall. He began in Baltimore on July 14, 1838, then moved to Philadelphia on July 23. The tour ended in Boston, where Catlin gave a series of lectures. He couldn't find space there for displaying the Indian Gallery until mid-September, when Boston's mayor gave him historic Faneuil Hall rent-free for a month. In October he was back in New York and the collection went into storage.

Catlin was at a crossroads. He was still corresponding with authorities in Washington, and occasionally making a trip there. But there was no progress. He had done no better than break even on expenses during the tour. He had made threats before to take the collection to Europe. Other Americans—James Fenimore Cooper and Washington Irving, for example—increased their reputations abroad. He would make one more try. He exhibited again in New York and Philadelphia. In both cities he announced that he was going to take the Indian Gallery to Europe. Newspaper editors took his bait. They expressed great disappointment that the government would allow the rare and prized collection to be sold to foreigners:

The New York Evening Star: *One of the most remarkable and interesting works that the genius and labor of an individual has created in this age and country . . . Nothing could rebound more to the patriotism, national pride, and honor of our country, than the purchase of this collection of Aboriginal Curiosities, to enrich a National Museum at Washington.*

The American Sentinel: *Mr. Catlin's extraordinary exhibition of Indian curiosities will be closed in a few days, as it will be taken to England at once and there disposed of. . . . No citizen should suffer it to leave this country.*

The United States Gazette: *Mr. Catlin has accomplished a work which will give him the highest rank on honor, with a subject that will interest the civilized world every year more and more through all time to come. We have learned with great regret that he will take his museum to England in a few weeks.*

Meanwhile, Catlin lowered his price to $60,000. The government was still not interested. There was no turning back now. He would look a fool and charlatan if he backed down on his threats. On November 25, 1839, the Indian Gallery—eight tons of strong chests and cases—was packed aboard the steamer *Roscious,* bound for Liverpool, England.

There was more praise in the New York newspapers when he left. But none were as effective as the simple words penned in a diary by Philip Hone, who had met Catlin at the exhibition:

Mr. Catlin, the Indian traveler, sailed on Monday last. . . . He will show the greatest and most interesting collection of the raw materials of America that has ever been seen on the other side of the Atlantic.

111

Catlin stood at the railing as the ship steamed out of New York harbor on a cold, blustery morning. He thought he might make money and a reputation in Europe, but his one great hope was that Congress might still act favorably and call him home to America. In his writings, he said nothing about the wife and daughter he left behind, or the second child that was expected. It would be a very long time before he saw his native country again. He returned an old, broken man, his life's work discredited.

The *Roscious* landed in Liverpool in January 1840. On the train taking him to London, Catlin was impressed:

> *The grandeur of the railroad stations we passed, the elegance and comfort of the cafés and restaurants we went to in the middle of the night, with the well-dressed, ruddy and substantial fellow-travelers, impressed me. I was of the conviction that I was in the midst of a world of comforts and luxuries. Surely people who can afford all this can surely afford a shilling apiece to view my Indian Gallery.*

Charles Murray, Catlin's friend from the days on the plains, was Master of the Queen's Household, and was of great help. He arranged for the lease on Egyptian Hall, a popular exhibition gallery. Catlin paid £550 (approximately $2,750) to rent three rooms for a year. The main gallery was 106 feet long, an excellent space to display paintings and other materials. Catlin knew this was the opportunity of his life, and wanted to outdo any exhibition ever seen in Europe.

More of his dwindling money went to have the front of Egyptian Hall painted, and its interior scrubbed and whitewashed. Carpenters put up racks and shelves and hung pictures under Catlin's direction. Gas lighting was installed. He had little money left after paying for handbills, catalogs, and the first installment on the rent. He seemed energetic and optimistic, but a terrible thought gnawed at him . . . becoming a showman might mean his death as an artist. He was too consumed by his mission, however, and had gone too far to stop now.

He had a private viewing attended by the Duke of Wellington, the Duke and Duchess of Sutherland, the Bishop of London, earls and countesses, and "ordinary Lords, Baronets, Knights and private literary, scientific and press gentlemen." Murray assured everyone that the portraits were authentic, pointing out chiefs and landscapes he had seen on his American travels.

The exhibition was opened to the public on February 1, 1840, admission one shilling. Great crowds poured into Egyptian Hall to view the exotic, fascinating displays. On the walls hung 485 portraits, landscapes, and scenes from Indian life. In the center of the room was a twenty-five-foot-high, white Crow teepee, with striking decorations of hunting and battle scenes. Hundreds of costumes, weapons, and domestic utensils were arranged on screens. Catlin answered questions during the day, and at night gave a formal lecture.

He was an instant success. No less satisfying to the self-proclaimed "backwoodsman from America" was his triumph in London society. Still handsome at forty-three, with an engaging charm and colorful stories, he was quickly taken up by fashionable people. He became as much an exhibit as the show. But he was happier than he had been in years, after the hard travel and work and self-denial, and the struggle with politicians. He wrote to his parents, barely able to conceal his pride:

I am well, though half-crazy with the bustle and excitement I have been under in this great and splendid city. . . . I have had the trembling excitements and fears which beset a greenhorn from the backwoods when making his debut to the most polite and fastidious part of the whole world. . . . I have kept as cool as possible—have pursued my course steadily and unflinchingly, and have at last succeeded in making what they call "a decided hit."

But as fast as the money came in, it went out for expenses, to repay a debt to his wife's family, and to carry on a social life he couldn't afford. It was the classic story of the innocent hitting sudden success and becoming overwhelmed by its pleasures. He was the darling of London society—little understanding that his celebrity would last only until a new sensation came along.

Clara and their two daughters arrived in London in late June 1840. Catlin had rented an expensive apartment in the most fashionable part of the city. "The coming of Clara with her two babies," he wrote, "was like the coming of the warm and gentle breeze of spring." But Catlin was worried. Attendance was falling at Egyptian Hall after months of peak crowds. He wrote to his father:

This is the "dull season" in London . . . all the fashionable are off to the Continent, the watering places, or gunning on their estates. There is a season for everything here, and the season for exhibitions has gone by. I am holding on with as much patience as I can. . . . The world may think I am making a fortune, and let them think so. But when I do make it, or any part of it, you shall know it.

He had the speculator's fever. His letters spoke of investment schemes, prospects for purchase, plans to exhibit in France, Russia, and other countries. But he was still fascinated by London society and the nobility. One letter described a reception he and Clara attended at Buckingham Palace:

> *To think from a little go-to-the-mill boy, I have worked my way across the Atlantic, and at last into the Palace and presence of the Queen of England. I received from her own lips her thanks for the interesting information which I have given her.*

Their third daughter, born in August 1841, was named Victoria, after the queen. To reduce living expenses, he moved his growing family to a small but comfortable cottage in Waltham Green, a London suburb. To revive interest in the Indian Gallery, he lectured at night by gaslight, with dummies in Indian costume to illustrate his talk. He soon replaced these with what he called *tableaux vivants*—twenty white men re-creating Indian dances and songs and war rituals. Later he would replace the white men with Iowa and Ojibway warriors visiting London. Little by little, he was adding the elements of the Wild West show that were so popular from the late 1800s to World War I.

TWELVE

DESPITE CATLIN'S NEW IDEAS, ATTENDANCE CONTIN-
ued to fall. He concentrated on publishing his book, *Letters and
Notes on the Manners, Customs, and Condition of the North American
Indians.* Washington Irving, the famous American writer, had given
Catlin a letter to John Murray, his British publisher. Enthusiastic
at first, Murray finally backed out, telling Catlin, "I love you too
much to take the profits of a book you risked your life for. Publish
it yourself—it would be too large a risk for me. But you can sell
enough subscriptions to the book at your exhibition to cover the
cost of publication." Catlin raised the money, and saved by doing
the layout himself, and managing the printing and distribution.

The monumental two-volume book was published in October
1841. It was an immediate success, highly praised by critics. Later
writers about Catlin lauded his achievement, but recognized its
faults.

Loyd Haberly's *Pursuit of the Horizon,* first published in 1948,
was one of the first Catlin biographies. He said the book was
"unbalanced . . . hasty . . . wordy . . . it conceals as well as re-
veals . . . full of needless digressions . . . sentimentality that seems

116

sickly now." But he concluded that "it has vivid descriptions, stirring incidents, pathos, delightful absurdities. It is the tale of a man, mindless of money and domesticity, following his own free will up and down dangerous rivers and through dangerous wilds, seeing everything, making friends everywhere, growing famous with confident ease."

William Truettner of the Smithsonian Institution summed up Catlin's accomplishment in his 1979 book *The Natural Man Observed*:

> *A curious blend of storytelling and perceptive reporting. . . . Its accuracy is questionable on many counts, and the chronology seems designed to confuse the reader. Yet* Letters and Notes *is one of the seminal texts of the period. Much of Plains Indian ethnology is still based on what Catlin observed and recorded.*
>
> *His descriptions of the endless prairie landscapes, wild chieftans and sacred tribal rituals, are as lucid and compelling as any to be found in journals of that phase of Western history. Nowhere does one find a more forceful exaltation of the American wilderness and its inhabitants, of nature and the natural order.*

Catlin made money on the book, but it didn't sell as well as he hoped, and expenses were heavy. The price was high, fifty shillings, and only two small editions were sold; he had to distribute through British and American publishers, and that cut into any profit. He wanted to return to America, but only on his own terms—when the government offered to buy the Indian Gallery. The crowds at Egyptian Hall grew smaller and smaller, and he didn't renew his lease for the third year. He decided to take his show on a brief tour of other cities.

Announcing the tour as his last before returning to America, he exhibited in Manchester, Edinburgh, Liverpool, and Dublin. He had promised Clara they were to sail for home in two weeks. But ever the optimist, he grabbed at yet another straw to renew interest in the show—and it proved disastrous.

In the spring of 1843 an unscrupulous promoter named Arthur Rankin came to England with nine Ojibways. He suggested to Catlin that real Indians would make the Indian Gallery an even bigger draw. Unknown to Catlin, Rankin had intended to exhibit the Indians himself, but was told he would fail unless they were under Catlin's management. The possibilities fired his imagination—the Ojibways would verify the truth of his paintings and lectures. He also thought it was his duty to protect their interests.

Despite Clara's pleading, he rented Egyptian Hall again for six months. She had always supported him, suffered his long absences without a murmur. This time she tried to resist, explaining that the Indians weren't his responsibility. Catlin, however, also saw a chance to make money before returning home. He made an agreement with Rankin: he would manage the exhibition, but Rankin was responsible for them offstage.

Dramatic and uninhibited, the Ojibways proved to be extremely popular and crowds once more filled the halls. They danced and stalked, yelled blood-curdling war cries, performed mock scalpings, and sang to the amazed audiences. The Ojibways even gave a command performance at Buckingham Palace for Queen Victoria and Prince Albert, her husband.

Charles Dickens attended an evening performance and was impressed with Catlin. He described him as energetic and earnest "while in all good faith he called upon his civilized audience to take notice of the Indians' symmetry and grace, their perfect limbs, and the exquisite expression of their pantomime. And his civilized audience, in all good faith, complied and admired." He was much less impressed by the Indians, describing them as "squatting and spitting . . . dancing their miserable jigs after their own dreary manner . . . mere animals and wretched creatures, and their dance no better than the chorus of an Italian Opera in England."

Catlin and Rankin divided a $400 profit every night. But after a month or two attendance fell again. Catlin was criticized for changing the nature of his Indian Gallery. He was also accused of exploiting the Indians, and the charge caused him great torment. And the Ojibways were causing trouble. They stood on the roof of the hall, and people in nearby houses tried to capture them before they "scalped" anyone. Mobs collected in the street and police were called. The Indians often mocked a nation they said was "ruled by a young woman." Then the Strong Wind married an English woman, and that caused a scandal. Another Ojibway told a newspaper reporter what they had seen in the streets of London:

Many people drinking. Five or six lying in the street like pigs. We saw much smoke and thought the prairies were on fire. There were many fine-looking squaws holding on to men's arms—and they did not look sick. We saw many, many people like a buffalo herd. Many people on the streets looked like they had nothing to eat.

Catlin argued with Rankin, who was supposed to care for the Ojibways when they weren't performing. Rankin suddenly took them away, saying he had learned enough to open his own show. He rented an adjoining room on the same floor and was competition for Catlin.

Only the birth of his son, George Jr., in November 1843 gave

Ball Play of the Choctaw—Ball Up. National Museum of American Art, Smithsonian Institution. Gift of Mrs. Joseph Harrison, Jr.

him any happiness. The boy was the joy of his life. He promised Clara that they would return to America as soon as his next book was published. *The North American Indian Portfolio,* a selection of hunting scenes, dances, and sporting contests, appeared in early 1844. Clara wrote home that they would be back by August.

Catlin changed his mind again when he met Mr. G. H. C. Melody, who was escorting a party of Iowas through Europe. Melody said he was given permission by the secretary of war to make the journey to improve the Iowas' habits and morals, as well as their simple minds. White Cloud, first chief of the Iowa, was the son of an old Catlin friend from earlier days on the plains. He couldn't resist the opportunity and made arrangements to reopen the show in Egyptian Hall. Deluding himself, he thought the Iowas, a proud and colorful group, might help him recoup his fortunes.

To bring the public something different, Catlin staged an outdoor display of the Iowas in London's Vauxhall Gardens. He had yelling Indians on horses galloping wildly about improvised teepees. He had only small success with the show, and took the Indians on a tour of other British cities. But the Iowas suffered from the damp cold and fell sick. Roman Nose and the small child of Little Wolf died of pneumonia in Liverpool. Catlin did all he could to keep the Indians healthy and comfortable, but he was desperate to recoup his losses. He felt that Britain had been "done out" for the show and took it to France.

He rented space in the Salle Valentino in Paris. King Louis Philippe was very interested in Indians and asked to meet the Iowas. He not only had bought Catlin's *Letters and Notes* and *Indian Portfolio,* but had traveled on the plains during his exile in the late 1790s. The publicity of that meeting made the public opening on

Little Wolf, a Famous Warrior. National Museum of American Art, Smithsonian Institution. Gift of Mrs. Joseph Harrison, Jr.

June 3, 1845, a great event. For a time Catlin again lived days of heady success. He met distinguished people: novelists George Sand and Victor Hugo, painter Eugene Delacroix, poet and critic Charles Baudelaire, and Baron Alexander von Humboldt, the German scientist. It seemed as if he had won all his gambles.

But the last blow to the homesick Iowas was the sudden death of Little Wolf's wife. They told Catlin they were going home from "this bad place" and sailed from Le Havre in July 1845. A certain reality finally struck Catlin. He was bone-tired, discouraged, and in poor health. Now he truly wanted to return to America and had just enough money to pay their passage. Then tragedy struck.

His wife's severe cold worsened into pneumonia. She died on July 28, 1845, only thirty-seven years old. Catlin was numb and bewildered and began to realize how much of his strength and spirit were hers. His grief and guilt were enormous. If he sometimes seemed callous toward his wife, he truly loved her. He was aware of the great sacrifices she had made for his career. Death, he thought, was probably the price of her worship and devotion. No relative or friend escorted her body across the Atlantic. Clara Gregory Catlin was buried in the family plot in Greenwood Cemetery in Brooklyn, New York.

Catlin vowed that he would soon take his children to America. But he was incorrigible—he took over another group of Ojibways recently arrived in Paris. They received a royal audience that so pleased the king, he offered Catlin gallery space in the Louvre museum. It was a stroke of luck because the lease on the Salle Valentino was about to end. Louis Philippe also said that France might buy his entire collection. He gave Catlin a commission for fifteen copies of subjects in the Indian Gallery for the Palace of Versailles.

At the close of the six-week exhibition in the Louvre, Catlin stored his collection and took the Ojibways to Belgium for a tour of Brussels, Antwerp, and Ghent. They got no farther than Brussels, where some Indians contracted smallpox and two died. Catlin brought the others back to England and never again attempted another live show. He returned to Paris and worked on the paintings for Louis Philippe.

Money was always a problem, but he couldn't deny his children anything. A governess cared for them, and the girls had a tutor for lessons and went to dancing school. They saw little of him except at dinner. Elizabeth, the eldest, haunted him because she looked so much like the dead Clara. When too pressed for money, he wrote to an English friend, asking help in the sale of the Indian Gallery to "the British Museum or some nobleman" for $35,000. He was almost certain he wouldn't earn much from the Louis Philippe paintings. "The compliment has been a very high one, but what the payment will be I don't yet know. Probably, like the honor, it will be a costly article."

In April 1846 he wrote to Congress, trying to sell the Indian Gallery for $65,000. He sent along testimonials from eminent American artists living abroad. While he waited, he painted and enjoyed young George. "He has adopted my painting room for his playhouse. Our happiness and enjoyment is mutual. . . . Besides the company of this dear little fellow, I had the sweet society of my three little girls." The children were his greatest concern. On fine days he took his laughing, chattering flock window-shopping along the grand boulevards of Paris. In the evening after dinner, they gathered around the fire and he told them breathtaking stories of the West.

He received a reply from the Joint Committee on the Library

of Congress. It proposed an amendment to the recent bill that established the Smithsonian Institution—the purchase of Catlin's collection would be included. But no action was taken. The tides in Catlin's life still ebbed. His children were taken sick with typhoid, and he spent every night at their bedside. Then his despair was almost suicidal. His adored son died of the fever in late summer. "And once again a broken heart," wrote Catlin. "Little George who had lived in the sweetness of his innocence, to gladden and then break the heart of his doting father . . . the remains of this dear little fellow were sent home to be buried with his mother."

THIRTEEN

HE WAS NOW PAST FIFTY, A MAN WHO HAD RISKED HIS family's health and happiness for his obsession— though he never once admitted it. Protective of his work with the Plains Indians, anxious to keep the glory for himself, he made another mistake. Henry Rowe Schoolcraft, an ethnologist and writer, received a grant from Congress for a major work on the North American Indians. He wanted to use many of Catlin's paintings to illustrate the book. He also had influence to get the stalled bill for the purchase of Catlin's collection passed. Catlin, however, felt confident he would get the sale without Schoolcraft's help and refused the offer. The book turned out to be a great success.

He finished the work for Louis Philippe, who was so pleased he ordered another twenty-nine at $100 apiece. They were to commemorate the explorations of Robert Cavalier La Salle in North America. It took Catlin almost a year to complete the set, but he was never paid. In 1848 revolution broke out in France and other European countries. Louis Philippe was deposed and fled the country with his wife. Because his relationship with the king was well-known, a mob broke into Catlin's studio on the Place

Madeleine. He managed to escape to England with his daughters and the collection, virtually penniless.

Spurred by his earlier success in London, he rented rooms at 6 Waterloo Place. They provided living space and a showroom. He worked on his Indian Gallery and now had 585 paintings in all. His troubles continued—he was growing deaf, his new exhibit drew few people, and the wealthy who once begged to buy his Indian paintings had mostly lost interest. Sir Thomas Phillipps bought a copy of an original, but refused Catlin's request for a $3,000 loan. Some time later he lent him $500 and received twenty originals as security.

In late 1848 Catlin published another book, *Eight Years' Travel and Residence in Europe.* It was written when he was nearly deranged with worry. The book was a failure, too rambling and windy, mostly a series of anecdotes about hobnobbing with European royalty. Year by year Catlin's reputation faded, and he was considered little more than an eccentric. His great accomplishments on the plains in the 1830s were still admired. But he had been too commercial and it tarnished him. In 1851 he painted fifty-five copies of his originals for Sir Thomas Phillips as payment of his debt. He also did drawings for another publication he called *Albums Unique.*

The next year he wrote to Congress again, offering the Indian Gallery for $50,000. It was a desperate move to save his collection and stay out of debtor's prison. By early 1852 Catlin's debts and bad investments caught up with him. He had lived on credit for years, borrowing against his collection, always gambling that the government would buy it. Creditors, he said, were at his door "like prairie wolves closing in on a sick old buffalo."

Kay-a-gis-gis, a Young Woman. National Museum of American Art, Smithsonian Institution. Gift of Mrs. Joseph Harrison, Jr.

All he had left were the three girls—and the regretful memory of his younger self so committed to a noble cause. At what point had he begun to chase money and fame? Sometimes late at night, when the children were sleeping, he slipped into the room where the paintings were hung. He lit a candle and raised it to illuminate the faces that were now his only true friends, and the prairies and rivers and hills that were his only true home.

Congress finally took action on the sale in the 1852–1853 session. It passed the House of Representatives, and with Daniel Webster leading the fight, passage in the Senate seemed certain. A powerful orator, Webster proclaimed the Indian Gallery "more important than all the drawings and representations on the face of the earth." Its purchase would be "an important public act."

Jefferson Davis, now a senator from Kentucky, praised his old friend from Comanche country. He said he had seen Catlin paint under the most trying conditions, and he was the only man to paint authentic Indians. Then he voted against the purchase—the deciding vote. He was a Southern Democrat and followed the party line. The South wanted Indian lands for the spread of slavery, and Davis couldn't support anything that would gain public sympathy for the Indians.

The Indian Gallery was seized by creditors and Catlin was thrown into debtor's prison. Small lots were put up for auction, but bids were so low the creditors looked for other ways to recover their money. His wife's family heard about Catlin's troubles and Dudley Gregory, his brother-in-law, sailed for England. He was a very rich man and could have paid off the debts, even built a museum for the collection. But Catlin was now looked on as a worthless father, responsible for the deaths of Clara and George Jr.

His financial collapse, his eccentricities, and his shame as a debtor forced the family's hand. Gregory took the three girls back to America where they could be properly raised. Before he left, he arranged Catlin's release from prison.

Catlin was so confident of the sale, he already had passage booked to Washington when he got the crushing news. When he discovered that his daughters were gone, he was near madness. He scurried about to escape bailiffs who still hounded him for payment. The rooms at Waterloo Place were stripped of all the paintings and furniture. The Indian Gallery was kept intact only by a stroke of luck.

Joseph Harrison, owner of a Philadelphia boiler works, was the largest manufacturer of locomotives in the world. He had just completed a $5 million contract to build a railroad in Russia. Passing through London en route home, the stocky, whiskered Harrison heard about the claims on the Indian Gallery. He paid off the largest debts against it for $40,000. To keep it from being seized or tied up by unknown creditors, he had the collection quickly crated and shipped to Philadelphia, where it was stored in the basement of the boiler works.

Catlin had lost everything but a few paintings, sketches, and notebooks he'd snatched from under the noses of the bailiffs. Somehow he got to Paris and took a cheap room on the Rue Tronchet. He was now fifty-seven, his hair was thinning and graying, his hearing getting worse. He tried to get some payment for the La Salle paintings done for Louis Philippe four years before. He was passed from office to office through the maze of French bureaucracy, and in the end gave up. His only comfort was that his collection was safe in America. He tried to work but his room was too cold and he couldn't afford firewood. More often he wandered the streets, a near-derelict, stopping at the fire of a chestnut vendor until chased away.

He often went to the Bibliotheque Imperial to get warm. It was much like a big city library in any era. Scholars and students studied texts. Obsessed "geniuses" wrote critical pamphlets against the accepted sciences. People's lips moved as they studied Latin, Hebrew, or Syriac. The desperately poor and homeless sat blank-eyed.

Catlin liked the atmosphere and the strange mix of companions. He enjoyed reading *Travels,* a new travel book on South America by Baron von Humboldt. He remembered that the great man had talked to him as an equal, eagerly questioning him about Plains Indian customs and language. Studying the book's maps, a new dream began to form.

The next day in the library, a grizzled man sitting nearby showed Catlin an old Spanish manuscript he'd translated. It told of fabulously rich gold mines discovered by Spanish explorers centuries before in Brazil's Crystal Mountains. Mysteriously, the man said, the mines had been abandoned to the native tribes. He read Catlin a short passage: "The Spanish miners, after accumulating great riches, were attacked by the Indians and massacred in their houses, or driven out of the country, leaving their gold behind them."

Catlin was fascinated, struck by the coincidence. Just the day before he was studying a map of Brazil. He loved the lore of any Indians and had always wanted to go to South America. But he quickly caught himself. He knew what travel tales could be—he had written some in his day. The long-buried lawyer in him looked for evidence of its truth. But the artist, adventurer, and dreamer in him was quickly convinced. The odds of finding the lost gold mines was a million to one. But he would never make enough money by other means to reclaim his Indian Gallery.

South America teemed with Indians. After all, he thought, he was only fifty-seven years old—he could paint another six hundred Indian pictures! He would redeem not only his Indian Gallery, but his good name! The port of Caracas, Venezuela, seemed the best starting place for his trek into the wilds. He slipped away from Paris like a fugitive after selling his last few precious paintings and sketches.

Using an assumed name, he got a British passport and sailed for Venezuela in 1853. He carried painting materials, a book of maps, notes, excerpts from von Humboldt's book, and a Colt repeating carbine. To get his aging legs in shape, he tramped the deck, hat pulled low and coat buttoned to the neck. It was a stormy voyage, but he stayed on deck and kept constant watch for the coast of South America. As the ship neared Caracas, he lifted his eyes to the green plateau beyond the red-roofed city and his heart pounded with excitement. He had come through every kind of hell, and once again his strength and determination had returned.

He joined up with a Dr. Hentz, a German botanist anxious to study jungle plant life. They went up the Orinoco River by canoe and steamboat to Georgetown, British Guiana. The trip took them through dazzling green distances and Catlin wrote, "Man begins to feel less than in England, his shadow is shorter." In Georgetown, a young Englishman named Smythe, equipped with a good rifle, asked to come along and Catlin agreed. The expedition now included Catlin, Smythe, Hentz and his servant, a half-breed guide, and a Spanish interpreter.

They spent some time in Paramaribo, Dutch Guiana, then went

up the Essequibo River by canoe with a family of Indians. The party hacked through tangled, dense jungle, slogged across swampland, and fought off jaguars, wild pigs, and snakes. Clouds of mosquitos, leeches, and ticks nearly drove them mad. But the lure of gold kept them going. The Crystal Mountains—and the fabled gold mines—lay deep in remote, unmapped country. But no matter how hard they pushed, the mountains always lay somewhere far beyond, and they soon realized they were lost. In a few days they reached Belém at the mouth of the Amazon River. Smythe, Hentz, and the others found the ordeal too great and quit. Only Catlin persisted in trying again.

He found a man named Caesar Bolla who had escaped slavery in Cuba. The big black man would become Catlin's faithful friend

A Man of Herculean Strength, Holding His Wife to Have Her Portrait Painted. American Museum of National History.

and assistant. They reached the Crystal Mountains, but lost their mining equipment in freak accidents. Catlin began to understand that gold had been a strong lure at first, but now it was a fantasy. There was something far more valuable to him in that magical country—hundreds of primitive tribes, far more mysterious than any he had yet seen.

The two wanderers crossed thousands of miles of wilderness far more difficult and dangerous than any in North America. Everywhere Catlin painted the Indians—Chetibo, Cocoma, Marahua, Iquito, Mayoruna, Omagua, Sepibo, Ticuna, Yahua, Angosture. Catlin used bristol board because canvas took too long to dry, and the steaming jungle turned it green with mold overnight. The thin white bristol boards were less bulky to carry and used far less of his precious paints.

Crossing the Mato Grosso jungle of Brazil, they went up the Amazon to its source in the Andes Mountains, then crossed into Peru. They traveled the pampas (plains) of Argentina, and journeyed all the way to Tierra del Fuego at the tip of the continent. Catlin and Caesar made passage around to the Pacific coast through the violent waters of Cape Horn. From Lima, Peru, they made their way to Panama, then to San Francisco on the schooner *Sally Anne*.

They sailed up the west coast of North America to the Aleutian Islands off Alaska and crossed the Bering Sea to Siberia. During the journey Catlin worked at a feverish pace, anxious to paint primitive life everywhere before it vanished. In the American Northwest he painted Klatsop, Chinook, Clickatat, Walla Walla, Nez Percé, and Spokane.

Catlin and Caesar went south to California, traveled inland and crossed the Rockies through the Santa Fe Pass to the Rio Grande.

135

Entrance to Lagoon Shore—
Lagoon of the Amazon. American Museum of Natural
History.

They paddled a canoe six hundred miles downriver to Matamoros, Mexico. From there they sailed to the Yucatan Peninsula, where Catlin wanted to study the ancient Mayan ruins. At Sisal in the Yucatan, the two friends parted. Caesar wanted to get back to Belém where he had fallen in love with a beautiful mulatto woman. As they shook hands, Caesar said, "Oh, Lord preserve you, good Mister Catlin! I will never forget you!"

FOURTEEN

IN LATE 1855 CATLIN RETURNED BRIEFLY TO LONDON, then went on to Berlin to visit Baron von Humboldt. They discussed Catlin's study of ocean currents and geology, and his theory of how they affected the movement of races. The scientists said Catlin should return to South America for more data and suggested places to go. Catlin embarked first for the West Indies to study tropical islands. In his cabin he found a note from the eighty-six-year-old von Humboldt. It ended "If I were a younger man I would join you in the expedition at once. I believe your discoveries will throw great light on the importance of natural disasters on the movement of races."

After the West Indies, Catlin explored Venezuela and Argentina. He and a man named José Alzar canoed up the Uruguay River. Catlin collected mineral specimens and painted Indians everywhere. But his age, sixty, was beginning to tell. Usually a dead shot, he missed a jaguar and the big cat almost clawed him to death. He recuperated in Buenos Aires, Argentina, then visited the Borrora, a tribe he thought rode as well as the Comanche and Crow. He was seen in Tierra del Fuego, then Peru and Panama—where he vanished for a long time.

The Handsome Dance (Gooagives) Venezuela. American Museum of Natural History.

There is no record of where he was or what he did for more than a year, but then he turned up in England. In 1861 he published *Life amongst the Indians,* a book for young people. Catlin had too many unhappy memories of England and moved to Belgium. He settled in a small apartment in Brussels and lived there as a recluse for the next ten years. The United States Consul in Brussels described Catlin at that time:

Quite robust and active for one of his advanced years . . . his hearing so impaired it was difficult to talk to him . . . his rooms were scantily furnished, and he lived in a frugal way . . . he seemed to have almost no acquaintances . . . He constantly expressed a hope that all his

140

works might be brought together and placed in the hands of the United States Government. He always took pride in calling himself "a friend of the Indian." He never mentioned his family, and gave no reason for the singular life he chose to live in Brussels.

Catlin wrote more books. *O-kee-pa,* published in 1867, was a description of the Mandan religious ceremony. The following year he published *Last Rambles amongst the Indians,* an account of his wanderings through South America and North America west of the Rockies. His last, in 1870, *The Lifted and Subsided Rocks of America,* presented his theories of geological phenomena observed during his 1850s travels. His one driving obsession was to reproduce the Indian Gallery lost to Joseph Harrison. Using notes, sketches, and his still vivid memories, he duplicated six hundred of the original paintings.

He still indulged himself in grandiose schemes and dreams. He planned a deluxe folio-sized catalog of the Indian subjects he'd redone. He hoped to print them by photo-lithography, then a new process, but that failed. He then planned a grand tour of Europe and Asia before making a triumphant return to America. His delusions were evident in dealings with the New York Historical Society. He offered to sell the original and duplicate collections for $120,000. It was another fantasy—he had no originals to sell. For eighteen years they had been stored in Harrison's Philadelphia boiler works. He had a small success with a last Brussels exhibition, and seemed, at last, to understand his situation. There was no further talk of grand tours or triumphant returns.

In 1870 he returned to a vastly different New York, anxious to see his daughters after more than fifteen years. He was seventy-four years old, wrinkled and deaf, but stood straight and proud at his last New York exhibition. The show drew only sparse crowds and closed quickly. People were no longer interested in Catlin and his Indians. He seemed little more than a relic from the country's past. Joseph Henry, the new secretary of the Smithsonian, invited Catlin to hang his paintings in the Washington, D.C., building.

Displayed so close to Congress, both men hoped it would renew interest in the Indian Gallery. But Congress, like the public, no longer considered the Indian a rightful inhabitant of the West. Expansion and white settlement had already crushed the fabric of Indian life beyond the Mississippi. Some congressmen asked why Catlin didn't just leave the paintings as a gift to the Smithsonian. They cared nothing that the paintings were only reconstructions—not even copies—of the originals.

Catlin was given the use of a small tower room in the Smithsonian. He continued to work until he became seriously ill with a kidney disease. Joseph Henry wrote to Dudley Gregory:

> *Mr. Catlin, although ill, is not confined to bed now . . . his physician has no hope for his recovery. . . . Mr. Catlin is not aware of the hopelessness, and the doctor thought it better to allow him to continue painting as long as his strength permits.*

Another letter followed two days later:

> *He has packed up his pictures to ship to his daughters in Jersey City . . . he has stopped work. . . . He is, although somewhat despondent, not in an unhappy state of mind. His life on the whole has been a successful one. He has succeeded in identifying his name with the history of the earliest inhabitants of this country, and is frequently*

George Catlin in Brussels. The National Portrait Gallery, Smithsonian Institution.

referred to in foreign works as the celebrated American ethnologist. In this branch of knowledge he is esteemed above anyone that has given attention to this subject.

Catlin was taken to Dudley Gregory's home in Jersey City, where his grown daughters cared for him and gave him the love and comforts he had missed for so many years. They said he was as stoic about his terrible pain "as any Indian." He tried to walk off his pain and helplessness until his scant strength gave out. . . . "If I was down in the valley of the Amazon I could walk off this weakness." Even as he lay dying, he was anxious about the fate of his collection. Almost his last words were, "What will happen to my gallery?"

George Catlin died early on the morning of December 23, 1872, at the age of seventy-six. He was buried alongside his wife and son in Greenwood Cemetery.

FIFTEEN

THE ORIGINAL INDIAN GALLERY WENT TO THE Smithsonian Institution in 1879. It was not by any act of Congress—but a gift to the nation by Joseph Harrison's heirs. During its many years of storage in the boiler works, many paintings, costumes, and artifacts were damaged by water, fire, rats, and moths. Most were carefully restored through the years, and about 450 of the original paintings survived.

Ironically, Congress's refusal to buy the Indian Gallery saved it. Had it gone to the Smithsonian before 1865, everything, every painting, would have been destroyed. In that year a great fire gutted the building.

There were better artists in the West of the early 1830s. Carl Bodmer and Alfred Jacob Miller were Europeans with excellent academic training. Their works—some of the same subjects and activities Catlin painted—were striking, technically superb. But as one critic said, "They painted beautiful pictures—Catlin painted Indians!" And no one ever painted them with more respect and sympathy.

Catlin was prophetic about the death of Plains Indian culture.

But even he was unaware how early it began. In 1842 a hundred settlers in eighteen wagons took off across the plains, marking a road later made famous as the Oregon Trail. It was not much at first—the grass probably sprang back in a week or so and erased the wheel tracks. But the next year a thousand came, driving five thousand head of cattle. From then on the trail swarmed with people and livestock.

For a century after, the Plains Indian was glorified and romanticized until he became *the* American Indian. In all the splendor of his eagle-feather war bonnet, he sits on his horse on a bluff, watching the covered wagons roll along far below. Suddenly he raises his rifle, the signal that brings a horde of shrieking horsemen down on the stouthearted pioneers. That image was a distortion. A stereotype created by a growing mass culture—dime novels, Wild West Shows, movies, television, and those lithographs of Custer's last stand distributed by breweries years ago.

Catlin's Indian paintings denied that stereotype of howling, bloodthirsty savages, killing for the sake of killing. They were people fighting to protect their homeland. He never denied their warring character, their plunder and cruelty. But his Indians were people with a true culture of their own. His paintings inspired almost every artist of the West. His writings influenced hundreds of ethnologists and writers. Americans saw his images reproduced countless times—but knew little of the man whose sacrifices and dedication created the work. Perhaps they caught the secret of Catlin's heart and that was his great appeal.

He seemed always possessed by a powerful nostalgia for lost innocence and tried to find it in unspoiled primitives. And it is that nostalgia—that search for the elemental dignity and authenticity in human beings—that so endears him to Americans.

BIBLIOGRAPHY

Catlin, George. *George Catlin's O-Kee-Pa*. New Haven: Yale University Press, 1967.

Ewers, John C. *Artists of the Old West*. New York: Doubleday & Company, 1973.

Haberly, Loyd. *Pursuit of the Horizon*. New York: Macmillan, 1948.

Hassrick, Royal B. *The George Catlin Book of American Indians*. New York: Promontory Press, 1981.

Haverstock, Mary S. *Indian Gallery: The Story of George Catlin*. New York: Four Winds Press, 1973.

The Letters of George Catlin and His Family: A Chronicle of the American West. Berkeley: University of California Press, 1966.

McCracken, Harold. *George Catlin and the Old Frontier*. New York: Dial Press, 1979.

Rossi, Paul A. and David C. Hunt. *The Art of the Old West*. New York: Alfred A. Knopf, 1971.

Truettner, William H. *The Natural Man Observed: A Study of Catlin's Indian Gallery*. Washington, D.C.: Smithsonian Institution Press, 1979.

Almost all of Catlin's paintings and collections are in the Smithsonian Institution, Washington, D.C., or, the Thomas Gilcrease Museum, Tulsa, Oklahoma.

INDEX

Index

Index

Index